BRAQUE

BRAQUE

EDWIN MULLINS

160 illustrations
31 in colour

THAMES AND HUDSON · LONDON

© EDWIN MULLINS 1968
PRINTED IN GREAT BRITAIN BY JARROLD AND SONS LTD, NORWICH

Contents

Preface

One of the questions facing an author who writes on Braque is how to date the paintings. Unwritten rules of art scholarship lay down that a picture should be dated to the year when the artist finished it. I have adhered to this rule, more in the absence of others more satisfactory than from any belief that it suits Braque especially well; for the artist would often work on a single painting for as long as a decade, adding the final touch perhaps many years after the main body of the picture was completed. As a result it is not surprising that in books and exhibition catalogues a number of key paintings have been given contradictory dates. This confusion was further thickened by Georges Braque himself who, as an old man, undertook to sign and date many of his early paintings – incorrectly. In such circumstances, and where other doubts have lingered, I have chosen to be consistent and to adopt the dating used in the illustrated catalogue being prepared by Madame S. Mangin of the Galerie Maeght in Paris, five volumes of which have already appeared.

To Madame Mangin, who allowed me the free run of her documentary material on several visits to Paris, and who obtained a great many photographs at considerable inconvenience to herself, I extend my special thanks. Among others who freely gave me their time and their help I wish to mention Braque's heir, Monsieur Claude Laurens, and that most gracious of dealers, the man who 'launched' Braque more than sixty years ago, Monsieur Daniel-Henry Kahnweiler of the Galerie Louise Leiris in Paris.

The directors of the Crane Kalman Gallery, Marlborough Fine Art Gallery and Redfern Gallery in London, and of the Galerie Beyeler in Basle, kindly supplied certain photographs.

Mr John Russell, himself the author of a book on Braque, was good enough to lend me the photograph of the artist reproduced in this book. To many museum directors and private collectors I also offer my gratitude for permission to reproduce works in their possession. Finally, my wife and many personal friends have helped probably more than they realize, by just listening and not looking bored while I talked. To them I wish to say 'Thank-you'.

Introduction

It is extraordinary that the closest and most productive partnership in twentieth-century art should have been formed by two men as diverse in temperament, in natural gifts, and in the overall direction of their careers, as the Frenchman Georges Braque and the Spaniard Pablo Picasso. Before 1907 their work possessed next to nothing in common. By the early 1920s it had again moved far apart. Yet for a few crowded years before the First World War their separate paths crossed – like searchlights from opposing camps – and at that point of contact sparked the first of the modern revolutions in art that belonged unequivocally to the twentieth century: Cubism.

Braque described this relationship with Picasso in suitably pioneering language: 'We were living in Montmartre, we saw each other every day. . . . We were like two mountaineers roped together.' On the one hand there was Picasso, a man forever among people, his ideas and passions drawn from relationships with people, his art amplifying the natural turbulence of his spirit, and reflecting always the urgency and the abundant variety of his human experience: on the other hand Braque, more solitary and reflective by nature, a man whose life and art were private, enclosed, whose range of experience was limited, a man among *things* more than people, for whom the world was a still-life, serene, unimpassioned, timeless, full of mystery, charged with indefinable subtleties of meaning.

To ask which of these two hit upon Cubism first is to pose one of those fruitless academic questions that will never be, need never be, answered. It is inconceivable that Braque would have ventured so boldly into the unknown without the example of Picasso. It is equally inconceivable that Picasso would have achieved those austere, delicate compositions of 1910 and 1911 without the example of Braque. For certain, it was the intuitive and irreverent genius of Picasso that supplied the drive and the iconoclasm: Braque's role was more passive, more pragmatic, adaptive rather than inventive, rational rather than impulsive. By nature Braque moved more slowly, resisted violent change, found Picasso's pace and daring as bewildering as it was stimulating. His reaction to Picasso's *Demoiselles d'Avignon,* Ill. 19 when he first met the Spaniard late in 1907, was one of undisguised shock, and he is reported (admittedly by a prejudiced witness, Picasso's friend Fernande Olivier) to have argued heatedly against the picture, declaring to Picasso, 'it is as if you wanted to make us eat old rope or drink paraffin'.

Yet within a matter of weeks Braque had himself begun a large canvas of a nude figure in which the dominant influence Ill. 17 was unmistakably that of Picasso's *Demoiselles,* and such a volte-face suggests a young man of impressionable, almost facile, adaptability. Indeed, only that October the large memorial exhibition of Cézanne at the Salon d'Automne had inspired another abrupt change; Braque had been instantly converted to Cézanne's geometrical style, as well as to his colour scheme. Moreover, this was barely two years since Braque had become the last convert to Fauvism.

For Braque, then, these were years of experiment. They were the only such years he was ever to undergo, and the Picasso-esque *Nude* was perhaps the least happy, least resolved, of these experiments. It is probably fair to say that Braque was not yet ready for Picasso. He was only just coming to terms with Cézanne in the winter of 1907, whereas Picasso in his *Demoiselles* had already adopted a conceptual approach to painting far more 'advanced' than Cézanne would have understood or approved. It was characteristic of Picasso that in so doing he should have by-passed Cézanne with a single intuitive foray, in the process – it may be said – outstripping himself almost as far as he outstripped his fellow-artists.

It was equally characteristic of Braque that the positive contributions he was soon to make to early Cubism should be not so much intuitive and experimental as systematic developments deriving from a profound and intelligent understanding of what had gone before: in particular a profound understanding of Cézanne. It was Braque who first consciously took up the spades Cézanne left behind. It was Braque whose respect for method, for order and for craftsmanship, supplied the counterpart to Picasso's mercurial brilliance. D.-H. Kahnweiler, at that time dealer to both painters, has written of the landscapes Braque painted in the year after his first encounter with Picasso, 'No connection existed between the two artists. This venture was a completely new one, totally different from Picasso's work of 1907; by an entirely different route Braque arrived at the same point as Picasso.' Kahnweiler was being a little premature in his assertion. 'The same point' (when their work became well-nigh indistinguishable) was not actually reached until the summer of 1911, when both men were working at Céret in the French Pyrenees.

CHAPTER ONE

Early years

On that first meeting with Picasso, the occasion when he argued so hotly against the *Demoiselles d'Avignon,* Braque was twenty-five, just six months younger than the Spaniard, and he had already lived in Paris seven years. Braque had come from Normandy, where since 1890 his father had run a successful painting and decorating business in Le Havre, the family having moved from Argenteuil-sur-Seine, outside Paris. It was at Argenteuil, the riverside village beloved by the Impressionists, that Georges Braque was born, on 13 May 1882. His father and grandfather were both 'Sunday painters', and it was with the full approval of his family that about 1897 Braque began to attend evening classes at the École des Beaux-Arts at Le Havre, where Raoul Dufy and Othon Friesz had studied a few years before him. Braque showed no precocious aptitude for painting and drawing, unlike Picasso, and his father seems to have insisted that his son at least qualify to practise the family profession. Accordingly Braque was apprenticed in 1899 to a local painter-decorator by the name of Roney.

It should be emphasized that to become a successful painter-decorator in northern France during the late nineteenth century involved acquiring certain skills that are no longer generally in demand. In particular it was essential to know how to imitate with the house-painter's comb various kinds of wood-panelling and marble surfaces. Such a style of interior décor was the rage among the *nouveaux riches* of the day, who were then building and furnishing elegant mansions for themselves in the prosperous ports along the Channel coast. This accomplishment, which Braque patiently learnt first in Le Havre and then in Paris (where he obtained his craftsman's diploma in 1901), endowed the painter with a respect for meticulous craftsmanship, and a sense of the value of decorative effects, which he was never to lose. Furthermore, it equipped him with an unusual skill which he was later to use (and teach Picasso to use) in his Cubist and post-Cubist paintings.

Braque continued to attend evening art classes after his move to Paris in 1900; but not until he had completed a short period of military service in 1902 did it become obvious to the young man that he would become a professional painter and not pursue his father's career. Supported by a small allowance from his parents he enrolled at the Académie Humbert in the boulevard Rochechouart, and in doing so – in ceasing to be an 'amateur' – he found himself joining in the regular company of young painters for the first time, forming early friendships with Francis Picabia and Marie Laurencin, and in particular with two slightly older contemporaries who had likewise come from Le Havre, Raoul Dufy and Othon Friesz. It was through these two painters that Braque was to become acquainted with the Fauve movement. He also began to frequent the Louvre, where he grew deeply impressed by the work of Poussin and Corot, and by Egyptian and Archaic Greek sculpture. At the dealers Vollard and Durand-Ruel, and at the recently displayed Caillebotte Bequest in the Musée de Luxembourg (the basis of the collection which now hangs in the Jeu de Paume) he became familiar with the Impressionists. He was also profoundly excited by the work of Van Gogh. 'What a great painter of the night', Braque was to say of him later (to John Richardson, *The Observer,* 1 December 1957).

Here was a veritable battery of influences in his first year as a full-time student. Again, though, it seems in character that for several years his own painting should remain relatively untouched by them. He waited until he had absorbed them thoroughly. Later in his life Braque destroyed a great many of *Ill. 2* his earliest canvases, but the few survivors, like *Breton Girl* and *Ill. 3* *View of the Park at Honfleur* make it clear that there was nothing startling or original about his work at this time; it was sombre in tone, conservative in composition, and remained faithful to

14

As a young painter Braque was not precocious like Picasso. These two works, done when Braque was in his early twenties, are both deeply in the mood of early Impressionism. They carry no more hint of the revolutionary to come than do the early landscapes of Mondrian. Braque himself destroyed a great many of these early pictures.

2 *Breton Girl* 1903–4

3 *View of the Park at Honfleur* 1904–5

4 *Boats* 1901–5

the spirit of early Monet, and of Corot and Boudin, whose works he would have known in the Musée des Beaux-Arts at Le Havre.

After two years at the Académie Humbert (broken by a brief and unsatisfactory spell in Léon Bonnat's class at the École des Beaux-Arts) Braque felt he had received enough formal instruction, and in 1904 took a Montmartre studio for himself in the rue d'Orsel. In the same year Picasso moved into a studio in the Bateau-Lavoir not far away. This was also the year when the first of a series of Cézanne exhibitions was held in Paris. Of all the influences upon Braque, that of Cézanne was to prove

5 *Ship in Harbour, Le Havre* 1905

the most formative and the most profound. For a while the influence of Cézanne was to be obscured by the impact of Matisse and by the Fauvist ideal of pure colour, which proved briefly and irresistibly attractive to the circle of young painters in the orbit of Matisse.

Yet already before the Fauvist diversion of 1906–7 there is present in Braque's work a serious concern to represent the volume of forms and the architecture of space. There was Cézanne in him before ever there was Matisse. *Ship in Harbour*, *Ill. 5* painted during the summer of 1905 spent at home in Le Havre, contains, it is true, hints of Fauvist colouring; but the really impressive advance this picture represents over Braque's work of the previous years does not lie here. It lies, rather, in the assurance (now considerably more than mere academic competence) with which he has balanced the heavy shadowy form of the ship jutting forward on the left, with the brightly-lit open area receding on the right. This is a painting which suggests Braque had already grown aware of the importance of Cézanne. Certain aspects of the picture, notably the blunt stabbed brush-strokes, also reveal a respect for Van Gogh – and for Seurat, a group of whose paintings had impressed Braque at the Salon des Indépendants in the spring of that year.

The Fauvist

In the three years that followed *Ship in Harbour* Braque's painting underwent a series of rapid transformations. This was the beginning of his experimental period. After his summer spent on the Normandy coast, Braque returned to Paris in the autumn of 1905 and was captivated by what had been derisorily labelled the 'Fauves' room at the Salon d'Automne, in particular by the work of Matisse and Derain painted that summer at the small Mediterranean port of Collioure, near Perpignan. These two painters, Braque said, 'opened the way for me.' The force and purity of their colours, the gusto of their approach to painting, their departure from conventional rules of perspective, their denial of Impressionist tonal qualities, all these opened Braque's eyes to a world of sunlight, of exuberance, of licence, in which the hand and the eye were free to interpret a subject as the spirit moved and as the surging of the blood demanded. Here was an intoxicating prospect, and it captivated Braque – briefly. It took him rather less than two years to realize that Matisse was inimitable, and that Fauvism as practised by his devotees offered – so to speak – the thrill of an orgy rather than of a love-affair; that beneath that thrill Fauvism obeyed strict and old-fashioned conventions of its own. Fauvism was Braque's first and last excursion into self-indulgence. Thereafter he was to follow the precept which he later summed up with the aphorism, written in the *Cahier* which he kept between 1917 and 1947, 'I love the rule which corrects the emotion.'

In March 1906 Braque made his first public appearance as an artist, contributing seven paintings to the Salon des Indépendants (all since destroyed); and in doing so he allied his sympathies firmly with the Fauvist group round Matisse. That summer he went to Antwerp with Othon Friesz, and here in a shared studio overlooking the River Scheldt he produced what he always considered to be his first truly creative work. As Fauvist paintings they remain tentative and cool, their bright red and blue highlights dabbed across the surface like the decorative bunting they so often describe. There is little in them of the full richness and vitality of Fauvist colouring which was to emerge in his Mediterranean landscapes. An exception is *The Mast, Antwerp*. Here the rhythmical and curvilinear patterns formed by the banks of clouds anticipate Braque's more inventive canvases done in the south a year later when Fauvism was truly in his veins.

Ill. 6

If the Antwerp pictures are the work of an apprentice who is learning fast, what Braque achieved during the winter of 1906–7 are the paintings of an artist enjoying his first maturity. After leaving Belgium in the autumn of 1906 Braque stayed briefly in Paris, visiting the Salon d'Automne which this year included an important group of paintings by Gauguin, before travelling on south to the fishing-port of L'Estaque, near Marseilles. There he remained until the following February. It was Braque's first visit to the Mediterranean, his first contact with the raw colours, the hard light and sharp contours of the south. Previously his Fauvism had been, as it were, second-hand. In Antwerp he had interpreted what he saw in accordance with his new admiration for Matisse and Derain: at L'Estaque he was able to appreciate for himself what Fauvism was about. A young man's art, Fauvism was essentially a response by northerners to the sun. It can be no coincidence that among the principal Fauvists only Marquet (born in Bordeaux) had been brought up in the southern half of France. It was an ecstatic response, one that took its cue from Matisse and from the appetite for Mediterranean landscape which had seized Van Gogh twenty years before. Braque was the last and the youngest of this particular group of northerners to indulge in that ecstasy.

He has said that he was at first blinded by the light and colour of Provence. But not for very long. Neither was Braque as blinded by it as were other followers of Matisse. Some of the

20

Ill. 7   paintings done in Provence late in 1906 (*e.g., Le Mas* and *At*
Ill. 8   *L'Estaque*) display a most un–Fauvist preoccupation with
solidity, with geometry, with a pattern of shapes organized to
fit tightly into the framework of the canvas; as well as an
interest in weight of shadow, and in a palette more sombre and
more delicate than was customary in the Fauve paintings of
Dufy, Vlaminck and Derain.

7 *Le Mas* 1906

shift of interest towards a more restrained and ordered approach to landscape is echoed in the following statement quoted by Georges Duthuit: 'It was impossible to make any further progress with the method adopted at that time. All those who have accomplished anything since have, to a greater or lesser degree according to their temperament, sought resistances. . . . You can't remain forever in a state of paroxysm.' When he departed from the Mediterranean that autumn, Braque left Fauvism behind him in the sun.

The influence of Signac's pointillism on Braque was short-lived, although he continued to use speckled areas as a decorative device most of his life.

10 *The Little Bay at La Ciotat* 1907

When Braque returned to the Mediterranean in May of that year (in Paris he had in the meantime become closely acquainted with Matisse, Vlaminck and Derain), first to La Ciotat and then to L'Estaque, his work began to acquire greater freedom and simplicity. *Hills at La Ciotat* and *Landscape at L'Estaque* are *Ills. 14, 12* characteristic. His work of that summer ranks among the most lyrical achievements of Fauvism. Yet, implicit in the strong

8 *At L'Estaque* 1906

9 *L'Estaque, L'Embarcadère* 1906

simple rhythms of these paintings lies a quest for something more substantial than Fauvism could offer: a quest for a formal orderliness, a discipline which would enable the painter to box a subject in, to bring it within reach and interpret it in terms of the flat surface of the canvas, without having to pay lip-service to perspective. In effect Braque painted these, his finest Fauve pictures, in a spirit of mounting disillusionment with Fauvism. He was already growing disenchanted with the ideas of Matisse. He has said that it was an increasing admiration for the Classicism of Ingres that was responsible for this break; and such a

◀ 11 *Port of Antwerp* 1906

◀ 12 *Landscape at L'Estaque* 1907

13 *La Ciotat* 1907

14 *Hills at La Ciotat* 1907

Braque had no consistent Fauvist style. These four pictures illustrate the range of his approach to landscape within a period of under two years. In the paintings of 1907 the interest shown in the rhythms of landscape is not characteristic of the other Fauvists, and seems to herald a wakening interest in Cézanne.

CHAPTER THREE

Towards Cubism

Paul Cézanne had died the previous year. It is reasonable to assume that Braque, like most of his contemporaries, was still no more than partially aware of the Aix master. This was to change dramatically with his return to Paris that October, where two encounters awaited him, both destined to affect his career radically. The first of these encounters was the double memorial exhibition of Cézanne – there were fifty-six paintings in the Salon d'Automne and seventy-nine watercolours at the Bernheim Jeune Gallery – which Braque visited shortly after his arrival in Paris. At much the same time he would certainly have read Cézanne's famous stricture, 'Treat nature in terms of the cylinder, the sphere and the cone', which occurred in the correspondence between Cézanne and Émile Bernard just published in *Mercure de France*.

From this moment Cézanne supplanted Gauguin as the master whom young painters in Paris most strongly admired. As for Braque, to appreciate the impact which these two exhibitions had on him it is only necessary to compare the Fauvist paintings he had completed at La Ciotat and L'Estaque that summer and autumn – in which the strongest influences are those of Matisse *Ill. 15* and Gauguin – with *View from the Hôtel Mistral, L'Estaque* which he painted shortly after seeing the Cézanne exhibitions a month or two later. They are in different worlds. In *View from the Hôtel Mistral* Braque has abandoned Fauvist colouring entirely in favour of a Cézannian palette of blues, greens and browns. He has abandoned all but the most cursory attempt at perspective in favour of geometrical patterns flattened in the manner of stage scenery. Most important of all he has painted the subject from memory. 'One day', he remarked later, 'I noticed that I could go on working at my motif no matter what the weather might

15 *View from the Hôtel Mistral, L'Estaque* 1907 ▶

be. I no longer needed the sun, for I took my light everywhere with me' (quoted by John Russell in his book on Braque, London 1959). It was a major step; for, unlike Picasso, Braque never possessed a gift for pictorial *rapportage*. His talent was perhaps too slow, too meditative. The impermanence of light, colour and shape in nature worried him. But from now on these problems dispersed.

View from the Hôtel Mistral was Braque's first confident step towards evolving a new plastic language – Cubism. Unknown to him, Picasso had already taken a more revolutionary step in a similar direction, by painting the large composition of five nude female figures known as the *Demoiselles d'Avignon,* which had occupied him for much of the previous winter and spring. Braque's painting was a methodical homage to Cézanne. Picasso's *Demoiselles,* on the other hand, was an intuitive leap into the unknown. It gathered into one painting heterogeneous elements derived not only from Cézanne, but from the massed figure compositions of El Greco, from early Iberian sculpture, Spanish Romanesque illuminations, and possibly from African tribal masks which the artist had by then begun to collect.

Ill. 19

The *Demoiselles* took Braque completely off his guard when, in the second decisive encounter of that autumn, he was taken by the poet and mouth-piece of the *avant-garde,* Guillaume Apollinaire, to meet Picasso in his Montmartre studio on the Place Ravignan. This meeting took place indirectly through a young German art dealer, D.-H. Kahnweiler, who earlier in the year had moved to Paris and opened a gallery in the rue Vignon (soon to be the Cubists' shop-window). A little while after the Cézanne retrospective exhibitions Kahnweiler called to see Braque and offered him a contract for everything he produced. He also introduced him to Apollinaire.

Ill. 17

Braque painted the large *Nude* during the winter of 1907–8, after the first encounter with Picasso. Like the major painting which preceded it, *View from the Hôtel Mistral,* the nude is heavily indebted to Cézanne. This is particularly true of the geometrical forms that fill the background to the central figure,

16 *Houses at L'Estaque* 1908

17 *Nude* 1907–8

18 *Nude* 1908

19 PABLO PICASSO
*Les Demoiselles
d'Avignon* 1907

The most immediate effect on Braque of seeing Picasso's great experimental canvas was to encourage him to make his own experiment with a figure composition, using the same unnaturalistic approach and the same broken-up planes. *Ill. 17* remains, all the same, closer stylistically to Cézanne than to Picasso. The impact of Picasso seems more clearly marked in the etching (*Ill. 18*) which he did a short while after. It is the first of his so-called Cubist etchings.

and of the clusters of parallel brush-strokes that describe each tilting plane. There are strong hints here of the enclosed Cézannian landscapes which Braque was to paint when he returned to L'Estaque during the spring and summer of 1908.

Besides the influence of Cézanne there is also the unmistakable impact of the *Demoiselles*. The nude figure is a rare theme in Braque's work, but it does recur at infrequent intervals during his career, and whenever it does so (I am thinking particularly of the *Canephori* of the 1920s and the *Bathers* of the early 1930s) it seems to be in response to an idea of Picasso's, an endeavour perhaps to come to terms with the Spaniard's vitality and inventiveness. Braque, so different in temperament, remained susceptible to Picasso's influence long after their association ceased. He was never so proud as to refuse to try out Picasso's ideas for himself, test them against his own talents, retain what was right for him. The *Nude* of 1907–8, painted so soon after Braque's violent reaction against the *Demoiselles,* was the first of many such occasions.

Ills. 71, 72

An interesting statement by Braque has survived (given to an American, Gelett Burgess, probably late in 1908 at the time of the artist's first exhibition at Kahnweiler's) which would seem to relate directly to the *Nude*. 'I couldn't portray a woman in all her natural loveliness,' Braque is quoted as saying, 'I haven't the skill. No one has. I must, therefore, create a new sort of beauty, the beauty that appears to me in terms of volume, of line, of mass, of weight, and through that beauty interpret my subjective impression. Nature is a mere pretext for decorative composition, plus sentiment. It suggests emotion, and I translate that emotion into art. I want to express the Absolute, not merely the factitious woman.' This statement appeared as part of an article published in the May 1910 issue of *The Architectural Record,* New York, under the title 'The Wild Men of Paris'. It is the first recorded statement in print by a Cubist artist.

On his third visit to the south in the spring and summer of 1908 Braque saw the Mediterranean landscape round L'Estaque

20 *Trees (at L'Estaque)* 1908

21 *Landscape at L'Estaque* 1908

Braque completed a series of enclosed woodland land-scapes which in some ways represent the climax of his fascination with Cézanne.

with very different eyes from those which, on his earlier visits, had drunk in the colour and dazzle of the Provençal country-side. In the past six months he had discovered Cézanne and discovered Picasso: and he had discovered that his interest lay in a *conceptual* approach to painting rather than in a *perceptual* one. In the landscapes of 1908 perspective has now been virtually eliminated by raising the angle of view and so cutting out the horizon altogether. It was a simple (rather evasive) solution to a basic problem. Fauvist colours, also, have quite gone in favour of a Cézannian palette of liquid green, yellow-brown and blue-grey; moreover these colours are no longer employed in an Impressionist manner, to describe light, but as an aid to defining and separating the geometrical forms into which a landscape may be simplified. Colour still plays a rudimentary descriptive role, in that yellow denotes earth and buildings, green denotes foliage, grey the trunks of trees, and so on; but there is no concern at all with the subtlety of light, or with the weight and texture of natural forms. What matters now is *shape*: how a landscape, once it has been depicted flat, may be seen to be constructed of so many discs, interleaved or welded together. Such was Braque's new vision of landscape, acquired through a study of Cézanne and through the impact of Picasso.

Thus the bulbous, curvilinear shapes of the Fauvist landscapes have given way to triangular and rectangular forms, as of a landscape quarried, or to diagonal scythe-like strokes cutting across and alternating with each other. Constructionally these

Ills. 20, 21 new landscapes of Braque are like a tent (Cézanne's late *Baigneuses* series may well have suggested this arch-like construction to him), the trees leaning first outwards to create a central volume, then the branches leaning in again to enfold above our heads, while the hollow centre – normally light in tone – recedes for a short distance only to be blocked off and the eye led upwards again to the vault of branches from which the entire composition appears to hang. This effect of a composition suspended so that it appears to be falling, while yet the eye is encouraged to look up at it, was to become a favourite

Cubist device of Braque's, of great assistance to him in breaking the convention of a single, fixed viewpoint. It culminates in the 1910 paintings *Violin and Pitcher* and *Violin and Palette,* which actually incorporate a realistic nail with a *trompe l'œil* shadow at the top of each picture, from which the composition appears to hang (see also page 56).

Ills. 35, 36

Already in the 1908 landscapes Braque has advanced a long way towards fulfilling the Cubist ideal of representing volume and space without traditional perspective and without anchoring the spectator to a single field of view. John Richardson, in *The Observer* of 1 December 1957, quotes Braque as proclaiming that 'the whole Renaissance tradition is antipathetic to me. The hard-and-fast rules of perspective which it succeeded in imposing on art were a ghastly mistake which it has taken four centuries to redress.'

In essence, though, Cubism was not to be an art of landscape: neither Braque nor Picasso was ever to be concerned primarily with landscape hereafter. During 1908 both men approached Cubism chiefly through landscape, and this was natural enough since landscape had been Cézanne's principal interest (handed to him by Corot and by the Impressionists) and in the early stages of Cubism it was Cézanne who was their guide. But once the grammar of Cubism had been established in 1908 – Braque working at L'Estaque in the south and Picasso at Créteil in the north – it grew increasingly obvious to both painters that the more natural development of this new pictorial language lay in treating themes which were close at hand and could be physically observed from all sides without a journey of fifty miles to do so. A multiple view of a vase clearly presented fewer problems to the painter than a multiple view of a mountain. In addition, the very proximity of an object to the painter all but removed the question of perspective and how to avoid it. So Cubism is *par excellence* the art concerned with enclosed and definable spaces, the art therefore of still-life. And Braque, long after his Cubist days were over, remained above all else a painter of still-life.

22 *The Mandolin* 1910

One of the masterpieces of Analytical Cubist painting, and of French still–life painting in general.

23 *Still–Life with Violin and Glass* 1913 ▶

It was during that summer of 1908, while he was engaged on Cézannian landscapes at L'Estaque, that Braque first began working on the still-life theme. *Still-Life with Fruit-dish and Plate* is probably among the very first of these. The arrangement of interlocking planes that block out the background is similar in composition to the landscapes of the same period, although the way he has painted the plate from above and the fruit-dish from one side is a somewhat crude device – cruder than anything in the landscapes of that year – for achieving the multiple viewpoint he sought. This kind of compositional problem seems to have solved itself when, after his return to Paris in the autumn of that year, Braque began painting still-lifes from memory (he had already done landscapes from memory).

Ill. 24

An early one of these was *Still-Life with Musical Instruments,* which he called his 'first Cubist still-life'. Here the physical volume of objects represented, and the space between and around them, are much more confidently suggested than in *Still-Life with Fruit-dish and Plate*: furthermore the background – and therefore any danger of creating an illusion of perspective – has been well-nigh eliminated by tilting the picture-plane until objects at the top of the picture appear to be as close to the eye as those at the base. We are looking, in effect, at a solid 'wall' of musical instruments: yet these instruments encompass and are separated by areas of space. At the same time the viewpoint is made to vary by means of a single distortion: the stem of the mandolin has been sharply bent so that the eye seems to be looking at it from on top and from below simultaneously. This was another device Braque was often to repeat.

Still-Life with Musical Instruments is a key picture in the evolution of Cubism, and it is perhaps Braque's first unquestioned masterpiece. It is also the first painting to illustrate what is probably the most important statement ever made by Braque (one that he reiterated frequently) concerning the way he came to see and represent objects, and how he imagined them to relate to himself and to each other. 'What particularly attracted me', he wrote '. . . was the materialization of this new space that

40

24 *Still-Life with Fruit-dish and Plate* 1908

I felt to be in the offing. So I began to concentrate on still-lifes, because in the still-life you have a tactile, I might almost say a manual space. . . . This answered to the hankering I have always had to touch things and not merely see them. It was this space that particularly attracted me, for this was the first concern of Cubism, the investigation of space. . . . In tactile space you measure the distance separating you from the object, whereas in visual space you measure the distance separating things from each other. This is what led me, long ago, from landscape to still-life.' It is evidence of the consistency of Braque's thought and aims that such an analysis remains as appropriate to the last

Braque's early
training as a house-
painter taught him
the skill, much in
demand at the turn of
the century, of
imitating wood-grain
by means of paint and
a comb. In the later
stages of Cubism, and
thereafter, he made
extensive use of this
technique. It gave to
his pictures a note of
fake realism which
appealed to him.

*26 Woman with
a Guitar* 1913

major achievements of his life, the *Studio* series of the 1940s and 1950s, as to these early Cubist still-lifes painted more than forty years before.

Braque was pleased enough with his work at L'Estaque that summer of 1908 to submit six paintings to the Paris Salon d'Automne. It was here, three years earlier, that Braque had been captivated by the famous 'Fauve' room. But to Braque's disgust the jury – who included Matisse, Rouault and Marquet – rejected the lot. Matisse proved decidedly less responsive to Braque's new ideas than Braque had been to the innovations of Matisse only a short time before; and the younger painter was bitterly disappointed. It was many years before Braque was to show again at any of the 'salons', and then only by invitation. After this rebuff Daniel Kahnweiler, his newly-acquired dealer, promptly arranged an exhibition of twenty-seven of Braque's paintings in his gallery at No. 28 rue Vignon, opening on 9 November. This was the first Cubist exhibition. It also provoked the first, half-derisory, use of the word 'cube' to describe the new style of painting which Braque and Picasso adopted. The critic Louis Vauxcelles borrowed the word from Matisse and in condescending language wrote as follows in *Gil Blas* (his review appeared above the news of a new record flying height by Wilbur Wright): 'M. Braque is an exceedingly bold young man. . . . He despises form and reduces everything, landscapes and figures and houses, to geometrical patterns, to cubes.' Monsieur Vauxcelles deserves a special corner reserved for him in the critics' pantheon, since it was also he who, with a similar half-concealed sneer, had been responsible at the Salon d'Automne of 1905 for coining the word 'Fauves'.

In general the bewildered disapproval of those critics who troubled to notice Braque's exhibition was in piquant contrast to the spray-shot of enthusiasm employed by Guillaume Apollinaire who contributed an introduction to the catalogue. 'This is Georges Braque,' he trumpeted. 'He leads an admirable life. He strives with passion towards beauty – and he attains it, apparently without effort. . . . A lyricism of colour, examples of

27 *Harbour in Normandy* 1909

which are all too rare, fills his work with a harmonious rapture and Saint Cecilia herself makes music on his musical instruments. . . . Purer than other men, he ignores everything foreign to his art, which might suddenly distract him from the paradise in which he lives.'

Gradually still-life was supplanting landscapes in Braque's output; and painting from memory was replacing painting

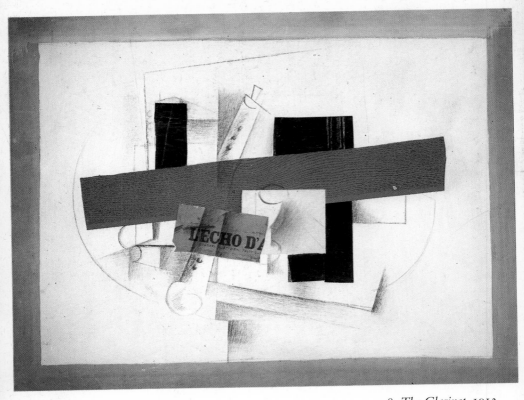

28 *The Clarinet* 1913

29 *Glass, Bottle and Newspaper* 1913 ▶

Ill. 27 directly from life. In the process the direct influence of Cézanne began to wane. Already *Harbour in Normandy*, which was an imaginary scene executed in Braque's Paris studio during the spring of 1909, answers less to the constructional principles formulated by Cézanne in the 1880s than it does to a new pictorial language of volume, light and touch. Douglas Cooper wrote of this important painting in the catalogue of the Arts Council exhibition held in Edinburgh and London during 1956,

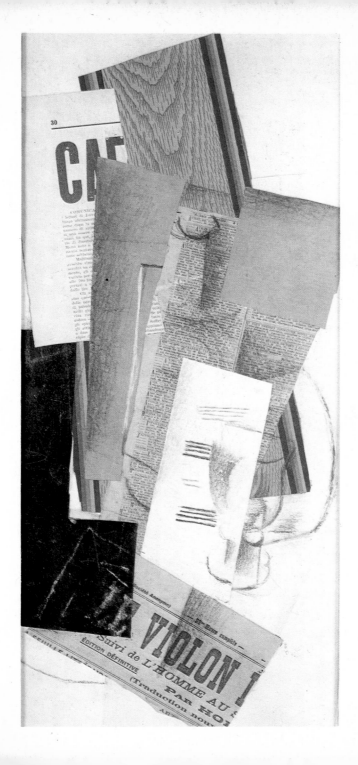

30 PAUL CÉZANNE *Village of Gardanne* 1885

'In this picture we see him feeling his way spatially round the hulls of the boats, the masts and the lighthouses . . . and then feeling his way out along the spars into the sky.' There are broad areas of space between hull and lighthouse, between mast and quayside, but there is no sense of distance.

In scientific terms space without distance – space being three-dimensional – may be a contradiction in terms; but the Cubists, dealing with the two-dimensional picture surface,

31 *La Roche-Guyon, the Château* 1909

were concerned with optical and not scientific truths. Braque, in maintaining that 'the whole Renaissance tradition is anti-pathetic to me', was objecting to the illusion whereby a two-dimensional surface masquerades as three-dimensional. His solution, and that of Picasso, was to substitute one illusion for another, the difference being that the Cubist illusion of tactile space without distance was, they considered, appropriate to the two-dimensional nature of the picture surface.

49

32 *La Roche-Guyon, the Château* 1909

In *Harbour in Normandy* everything has been brought forward to the touch, like braille. As a result the picture is only a landscape in name. Where there is no distance, after all, the concept of landscape ceases to exist. The lighthouses here might equally well be pepper-pots, the ships sauce-boats, and the title 'Still-Life on a Table'. Altogether Braque's growing affection for the still-life theme over the forthcoming years represents, as this painting indicates, not so much the shutting out of the wider world as the embracing of it, bringing it all within reach.

Braque did have one final summer working directly from life. While Picasso was in Spain painting landscapes at Horta, Braque spent the early part of the summer of 1909 in the hill-town of La Roche-Guyon, on the Seine. Like Cadaquès (which Picasso photographed as if to prove the point – see Edward Fry's *Cubism*), La Roche-Guyon was a ready-made Cubist subject. That is to say, it was composed of a geometrical pattern of small houses straggling up the hillside, with neither sky nor horizon behind them for the artist to dispose of. It is likely that Braque was beckoned there by the knowledge that in La Roche-Guyon Cézanne had painted some of his most advanced constructional landscapes during a stay with Renoir twenty-four years earlier. (Cézanne had then gone south to Gardanne, and a group of his landscapes painted there bear a strong similarity to the paintings Braque did of La Roche-Guyon.) The predominantly green and buff colour scheme of the eight landscapes Braque produced there that summer even suggest a last leave-taking of Cézanne, a final tribute to a master and guide before striking out on a path with Picasso which was to lead far from any territory Cézanne would have recognized or approved. The La Roche-Guyon paintings are the climax of Braque's Cézannian Cubism. And except for a study of the Sacré-Cœur and a few studies of Céret done the following summer – the latter scarcely distinguishable as landscapes anyway – they mark the end of his interest in landscape for almost twenty years.

Ill. 30
Ills. 31, 32

51

CHAPTER FOUR

Analytical Cubism

A brief period with Derain at Carrières-Saint-Denis followed the stay at La Roche-Guyon in the late summer of 1909, after which Braque returned to Paris. This was the autumn of his ripening friendship with Picasso; the autumn of Analytical Cubism; the autumn too of Braque's introduction to the figure paintings of Corot. Until twenty-four of these were exhibited at the 1909 Salon d'Automne they were a relatively unknown aspect of a man still popularly regarded as the mass-producer of twilight rhapsodies for the American market. There is evidence in many of the earliest of Braque's paintings that he had always held Corot in high esteem. It is difficult to believe that a picture

Ill. 2   like, for example, *Breton Girl* of 1903–4 could have been painted without some acquaintance with the work of Corot, and a profound feeling for it. The influence of Corot upon Cubism has never been properly examined. Indeed, few stylistic links support any such view; yet it is unlikely to be a coincidence that Braque's brush-work grew increasingly feathery and delicate during the two years following the 1909 Corot exhibition at the Salon d'Automne; or that during the same period he paid the closest attention to the quality of his greys and whites; or that one of Braque's favourite Cubist themes should also have been one of Corot's favourite themes – a figure holding a musical instrument; or that the reproduction pinned to the wall of Braque's studio for so many years should have been of Corot's

Ill. 69   *Portrait of Christine Nilsson,* much later to be the inspiration of
Ill. 70   Braque's own *Souvenir de Corot.* Corot-esque qualities are never more conspicuous in Braque's work than in the Analytical compositions painted between late 1909 and 1912.

One of the earliest 'analytical' paintings, as well as one of the
Ill. 33   most beautiful, is *Guitar and Fruit-dish,* executed probably

33 *Guitar and Fruit-dish* 1909

during the autumn of 1909. Here a group of objects already familiar from Braque's earlier still-lifes is described by means of the softest variations of buff and grey. Each image is firmly outlined in a darker shade – this was to become a characteristic of Braque's still-lifes – and within a scaffolding of diagonal lines each plane is suggested by a now-familiar passage of parallel brush-strokes moving softly from dark to light. By these means the impression is created that each flat surface is tilting, that the play of light upon them is varying continuously, and that the angle of view, instead of being fixed, shifts as the eye wanders over the picture. The delicate pallor of its colouring, and the pervading tranquillity of its mood, are reminiscent of Corot, but in the tenderness Braque has managed to impart to ordinary household objects one is reminded of another French master a century earlier than Corot: Chardin. Together with the La Roche-Guyon landscapes, this picture marks a climax of Braque's so-called Cézannian period, and at the same time it looks forward to the more complex treatment of light and of volumes which Braque was to employ in the still-lifes painted early the following year at the height of Analytical Cubism, such as *The Mandolin*.

Ill. 22

The term 'Analytical Cubism' was coined by Juan Gris, the young Spanish painter who was soon to become the junior member of the Cubist trio. He used it to describe the paintings done by Picasso and Braque during the period beginning in the late autumn of 1909. Since their return to Paris after the summer, both Braque and Picasso now had studios in Montmartre, and used to see one another each day. Kahnweiler recalls how almost every evening, after a day's work, Picasso would call for Braque on his way down the hill, and they would then drop into his gallery for a chat. By now the two painters were working virtually in harness: each followed the other's ideas and progress with such care that their work grew increasingly alike. It was the beginning of the most remarkable partnership in modern painting, in which the two artists were (in Braque's phrase) 'like two mountaineers roped together'.

Braque's paintings done during this winter of 1909–10 have the appearance of images reflected in shattered glass. Shapes are broken up rather than destroyed. There is still no loss of identity, although it often involves an intensive search to find the images contained in them. Unlike the paintings of the 'Hermetic'

34 *View of Montmartre (with Sacré-Cœur) from the Artist's Studio* 1910

phase of Cubism to follow, the pictures of 1909–10 are still intended to be 'read'. 'When objects shattered into fragments appeared in my painting about 1909', he recalled later, 'this for me was a way of getting closest to the object. . . . Fragmentation helped me to establish space and movement in space.' Often, as in *Violin and Pitcher,* he made use of strong effects of lighting *Ill. 35* playing from several sources at once. This assisted the process of fragmentation, helped to emphasize the nature of the different volumes and to pick out the pools of space lying between those volumes. The colour scheme is invariably neutral – an almost *grisaille* palette – because as Braque has explained 'colour could give rise to sensations which would interfere with our conception of space'.

35 *Violin and Pitcher* 1910

36 *Violin and Palette* 1910

37 *Piano and Lute* 1910

Cubism reached its apotheosis in the portraits by Picasso (*Ill. 41*) and the large upright still-life compositions of Braque. Even Braque's figure-studies of the period (*e.g. Ills. 39, 42* and *44*) are in effect still-lifes.

What Braque meant by 'our conception of space' was a two-dimensional interpretation of it achieved by fragmenting and analyzing volumes, rather than the traditional interpretation achieved by presenting an illusion of distance through the use of perspective. And as if to demonstrate the difference between these two solutions, Braque included in two paintings done *Ills. 35, 36* during this winter (*Violin and Pitcher* and *Violin and Palette*) the naturalistic image of a nail, complete with *trompe l'œil* shadow, at the top of each picture. It was a didactic touch; and a bit of a joke no doubt. It served, as well, to emphasize a vertical arrangement of forms suspended, so to speak, from the top of the

56

picture-area rather than built up from the base as would
normally be the case in a still-life. Besides, the nail was almost
certainly a deliberately introduced incongruity; something
designed to perplex the eye, to disturb the mind, to introduce
an element of mystification, all of which Braque came to regard
later in his career as essential ingredients of a good picture. An
element of mystery, he considered, formed an indispensable
barrier between the spectator and his dangerous tendency to
interpret a painting *literally,* to demand of every shape, every
image and every brush-stroke that it stand for an equivalent in
life and answer to a precise meaning explicable in words. The

incongruous element preserved, for Braque, the authority of the artist's conceptual interpretation of the world – an interpretation that was indefinable in terms of words and indefinable in terms of naturalism – which reached its apogee in the *Studio* series of the late '40s and '50s.

A great many twentieth-century painters, from Picasso to Jasper Johns, have been similarly interested in the distinction between the image in life and the same image in paint, Johns in particular having sought to explore the strip of no-man's-land in which the two can become most readily confused. Unexpectedly Braque anticipates Johns here. Lacking the genius for caricature which led Picasso so far from naturalism, Braque – like Johns – treated humble and everyday images in a straightforward and loving manner which seems to invite a literal interpretation only to dispel it. Braque's illusionistic nail is an archetypal Johns image, just as Johns's coat-hangers and numbers are pure Braque, even to the painterliness of them. It is a surprising link.

Ill. 22
Ill. 33 Only a few months separate *The Mandolin,* painted during the winter of 1909–10, from *Guitar and Fruit-dish* of the previous autumn. In both pictures the angle and position of the musical instrument is much the same, but in the later work it is no longer distorted simply to examine and throw emphasis upon its volume. Instead the instrument has been taken to pieces and reassembled out of numerous rectangular or irregular-shaped facets, like small cut-out templets. Braque, in short, has begun to take much freer liberties with his subject, and the effect here is to make the instrument merge into its surroundings, instead of standing freely from them as in the earlier painting. This blending of image and background has enabled Braque to achieve, in *The Mandolin,* the maximum sensation of space without creating the impression that any one area of the painting is further from the eye than any other.

Conspicuous in *The Mandolin,* too, is the tendency to fade away at the corners of the painting. This achieves, in effect, an oval format within a rectangular one. The format within a

38 *Glass on a Table* 1910

format becomes even more evident in a still-life painted a month
or so later, *Glass on a Table*. The next stage was that Braque on   *Ill. 38*
occasions cut out the corners altogether, with the result that an
important body of his Cubist work in the next few years
became oval-shaped. One of the earliest and finest of these,
painted early in 1910, is the large figure composition *Woman*

59

Ill. 39   *with a Mandolin.* Here the outer areas on the left and right are made up of lyrical passages of paint that serve no descriptive purpose; they merely guide the eye pleasantly enough towards the upright figure in the centre. Like the other large figure studies Braque painted during 1910 and 1911, this is in no sense a portrait: the figure is as much an impersonal object as the mandolin she plays. She is a woman but not a person: the

39 *Woman with a Mandolin* 1910

40 *Violin and Glass* 1910–11

human theme supplies no more than a formal coherence to a complex arrangement of planes and volumes.

How unlike Picasso this is. Even at a time when stylistically their work was drawing so close as to be almost indistinguishable, a fundamental difference between their treatment of figures exposes the gulf that lay between the two men. Picasso's fascination for people's individual traits of personality, plus his

41 PABLO PICASSO
Portrait of Daniel-Henry Kahnweiler
1910

Picasso had a love
of portraiture
which Braque
never shared.
Even at the height
of Analytical Cubism,
when impersonality
held sway,
Picasso never
lost sight of what was
individual in a face or
a bearing.
It was portraits
like this one –
Kahnweiler was the
Paris dealer for both
artists at the time –
that led Braque
to try his hand at
Cubist figure
compositions.

Ill. 41

natural gift for portraiture and for slightly malicious caricature; these qualities ensure that Picasso's Analytical Cubist portraits (those of Vollard and Kahnweiler are among the best) really are portraits: each is a witty, somehow profound study of a particular man's appearance and character. Braque on the other hand possessed neither an interest in portraiture nor a gift for it. What distinguished one person from another was of no more importance to him as a painter than what distinguished one lemon from another. They were human forms, and that was enough.

In *Woman with a Mandolin* the technique of moving from *Ill. 39* dark to light within each plane remains precisely the same as he was employing in his landscapes and still-lifes of 1909 (except that now the brush-strokes tend to be in shorter stabs), but it has become clear that the diagonal and horizontal lines which pervade the canvas not only have the function of defining each physical plane, they are also used non-descriptively to link one plane to another. They are imaginary guide-lines tracing the divisions of light and shade, without any direct relation to a physical object. Colours, too, are now far from being the natural colours of the images represented. Just as planes have begun to be dissociated from physical volumes, so colours have been freed from their 'local' or descriptive functions; and these trends become a great deal more pronounced in the series of major compositions which Braque was working on during the following year, 1911. Pre-eminent among these are *The* *Ills. 42, 44,* *Portuguese, Woman Reading, The Guéridon* and *Man with a Violin.* *46, 47*

The isolation in which Braque and Picasso were working during these years (and it was an isolation as much from other artists – even from those beginning to work on similar lines such as Gleizes, Metzinger, Léger and Le Fauconnier – as from the critics and the general public) tends to be obscured by the *succès de scandale* which Cubism enjoyed, and by the extra-ordinary influence it exerted on scores of young artists only a year or two later. Amid a climate of incomprehension and hostility, from 1909 onwards both Braque and Picasso ceased to send paintings to either of the annual open exhibitions of contemporary painting, the Salon des Indépendants and the Salon d'Automne, and showed their work only with their youthful and open-minded dealer, D.-H. Kahnweiler. As a result, it is a curious fact that all the noisiest early manifestations of Cubism, in particular the *Section d'Or* exhibition held at the Galerie de la Boétie in Paris during October 1912, took place without the participation of the two founders and principal exponents of Cubism. It was disciples like Metzinger and Gleizes, whose paintings echoed their fascination for the intellectual and theoretical aspects of the new art, who earned the first public acclaim – and derision – for practising it.

It should be recognized, all the same, that it was from within this circle of disciples that some of the first intelligent explanations of Cubism reached the eyes of the public. Metzinger and Gleizes wrote the first book on Cubism (in 1912); two years earlier Metzinger had paid an effusively chauvinistic tribute to Braque, in the October–November issue of *Pan*. 'Braque', he wrote, 'joyfully fashioning new plastic signs, commits not a

42 *The Portuguese* 1911

single fault of taste. . . . I can compare him to Chardin and Lancret: I can link the daring grace of his art with the genius of our race.' Other writers were to make valuable early contributions to the de-mystification of Cubism. Maurice Raynal, writing a catalogue preface for the Rouen *Salon de juin* in 1912, pronounced: 'The élite of today rightly considers that the artist, at the same time as he sees, must conceive the object he proposes to represent.' In the same year André Salmon wrote with cool accuracy in *La Jeune Peinture Française*, 'Cubism will

43 *Still-Life with Violin* 1910–11

44 *Woman Reading* 1911

at least have restored the cult of method.' The indefatigable Guillaume Apollinaire, writing in *Le Temps* for October 1912, defined Cubism in more penetrating terms as 'the art of painting new wholes with elements taken, not from the reality of vision, but from the reality of conception'. And in the Munich *Der Blaue Reiter*, also 1912, Roger Allard answered his own question 'What is Cubism?' with the verdict 'First and foremost the conscious determination to re-establish in painting the knowledge of mass, volume and weight.'

Superficially it might appear that in 1910 and 1911 Braque – Picasso too – was heading directly for abstraction. Had this in fact occurred it is not hard to envisage today a chorus of art historians chanting that abstraction was of course implicit in such paintings as *Woman with a Mandolin* and *The Portuguese*: indeed, what more appropriate moment for this to have occurred, it might have been argued, just when in Munich Kandinsky was losing faith in representational landscape, when in Paris Delaunay and Kupka were beginning their researches into colour-abstraction, and in Russia Malevich and El Lissitzky were conducting their first experiments with small black and white constructional forms? Yet an abstract ideal, in which colour and form could be dissociated entirely from any real or recognizable image (not merely separated from it), was totally in opposition to the aims which both Picasso and Braque were pursuing. The very nature of Cubism, and the course Braque and Picasso were following, was dictated by the reverse ambition, namely to approach real objects as closely as possible, and to convey by means of paint on a flat surface a living experience of actual and tangible things.

Cubism is about physical facts, and the human experience of those facts. What does seem to have happened is that, as images became increasingly fragmented, and as colours, lines and even forms became freed from a directly descriptive function, both painters began to sense the dangers of abstraction, and to take measures to avoid them. The development of Cubism, from its so-called 'Hermetic' phase in 1911 until the First World War

66

broke up the partnership between the two painters, was to a great extent determined by the need which both of them recognized to keep their work in touch with the reality upon which it fed. In a sense the mountain which they had been steadily climbing together from 1909 was at several moments seen to be leading into the clouds, and several abrupt alterations of direction became essential if all contact with the living world was not to be lost.

As in 1909, Braque and Picasso had spent the summer of 1910 working apart, Braque at L'Estaque once again, Picasso at Cadaquès on the Costa Brava with Derain. But in the summer of 1911, the year when their paintings grew so alike that often it is barely possible to distinguish one man's work from the other's, they worked together at Céret in the French Pyrenees, not returning to Paris until October. It is probable that the example and influence of Picasso, who had painted several large Cubist portraits during his stay at Cadaquès the previous year, was what encouraged Braque to concentrate on large figure subjects while he was at Céret; and the results are among the most majestic products of Cubism, as well as being some of the most important works of Braque's long career.

The Portuguese, painted early in 1911, possesses many of the features already noticed in *Woman with a Mandolin* of a year earlier. Again he has taken the theme of a musician: again (although not this time oval in format) the composition is upright, with a preponderance of downward-sloping lines which convey the impression of a form suspended from above like a robe (a favourite device of Braque's since the Cézannian landscapes of 1908, and particularly noticeable in the two still-lifes of 1910, *Violin and Palette* and *Violin and Pitcher*). Again, too, effects of space and volume are achieved by planes that progress systematically from dark to light, each plane thinly outlined in black. But now the stabbed brush-strokes are shorter – almost *pointilliste* in technique – the colours cooler and paler, the figure even more fragmented and difficult to identify, and the composition altogether more linear; while a high proportion of lines

Ill. 42

Ills. 35, 36

now no longer relate physically to the figure itself, but either pick out isolated motifs scattered here and there, or measure distances between one form and another, or serve to organize and distribute the fall of light round the figure as if covering it with the complicated folds of a veil.

At the same time, perhaps to counteract the trend towards obscurity, Braque has added a new realistic touch. He has painted in letters from the *Grand Bal* poster on the wall of the Marseilles bar where he had originally seen the musician. 'I started to introduce letters into my pictures', Braque has explained. 'These were forms which could not be deformed, because, being two-dimensional, they existed outside three-dimensional space; their inclusion in a picture allowed a distinction to be made between objects which were situated in space and those which belonged outside space.' Combining what was literally real with a personal interpretation of what was real – objectivity with subjectivity – was to become in the work of both Picasso and Braque the most prominent feature of their last Synthetic phase of Cubism. It is another indication of Braque's lifelong affection for the incongruous: his love of the puzzle which disturbs.

Many of the fresh developments in style noticeable in *The Portuguese* are more strongly pronounced in Braque's figure compositions done later that year. In *Woman Reading,* painted at Céret during the summer, the actual figure of the woman has all but disappeared. One can pick out her hair at the top of the picture, and what look like her legs at the base of it (or is it the book she is reading?). Otherwise, apart from portions of the chair on which she sits, description has been now virtually replaced by a geometrical network of lines that probe, measure, pick up a shape here and there, divide areas of light from areas of shadow, act as guide-lines for the eye to trace the general shape and movement of the composition. Even the planes are no longer clearly divided, but drift into and over one another independent of the outlines which formerly defined them. A systematic alternation of pale with dark areas has now given way

Ill. 44

68

to a more diffused stipple of light and heavy tones, and to an overall progression from dark at the extremities of the picture to pale at the centre. Braque never paid closer attention to the elegant subtleties of his brush-work than at this moment in his career.

One of Braque's first engravings, *Fox,* which Kahnweiler   *Ill. 45*
commissioned from the artist during the same year, 1911, supplies what is possibly the clearest insight into Braque's ideas and working method at this time. Like the important group of

45 *Fox* 1911

46 *The Guéridon* 1911

47 *Man with a Violin*
1911–12

48 *Still-Life with Dice,
Pipe and Glasses* 1911–12

70

ten Cubist etchings Braque did at this time, *Fox* resembles the black and white (*i.e.*, constructional) areas of one of his contemporary paintings. The surface is dotted and rubbed with little disconnected lines, numbers, patches of shade, recurring fragments of motif, marks of emphasis and reference; and the composition has obviously been built up bit by bit rather than conceived as a whole. A painting in the Rupf Foundation in Berne, *Bottle and Glass,* shows how this composition has become the basis of a picture (it might possibly be the other way round – Braque left no clues); and a similar constructional method is responsible for another of Braque's large figure compositions of that year, *Man with a Violin,* and the large still- life *The Guéridon* in which a veritable jumble of fragmented motifs is piled upon a more easily recognizable circular table.

Ill. 47
Ill. 46

71

CHAPTER FIVE

Synthetic Cubism

It has already been suggested that the introduction of lettering taken from posters and labels, in paintings such as *The Portuguese* of 1911, introduced an element of literal everyday realism (one is tempted to say an element of Pop Art) to what was threatening to become dangerously obscure. Guillaume Apollinaire was quick to understand the point of this development. In the magazine *Der Sturm* of February 1913, he wrote 'Picasso and Braque incorporated in some of their pictures letters from labels and other printed matter, because label, notice and advertisement play a very important aesthetic role in the modern city and are well-suited for incorporation into works of art.'

In the year 1912, Braque delved into his youthful apprenticeship as a painter-decorator for another touch of realism: he began to introduce areas of paint that imitated wood-panelling, using the same skills with the house-painter's comb as his father had so successfully practised in the Normandy houses of the *nouveaux riches* during the latter part of the nineteenth century. André Salmon, writing in *La Jeune Peinture Française* some years later (1919), commented of Braque: 'His family painted, or saw to the painting of, the interior walls of nearly all the buildings constructed in Le Havre at the end of the last century. I am convinced that Georges Braque owes some of his most brilliant qualities to his descent from such a family.'

Ill. 49 At first this new feature appears shyly, in a relatively insignificant bottom-left corner of *Homage to J. S. Bach* painted during the spring of 1912. But within a year it had grown into an important factor in his work (for example, *Still-Life with* *Ill. 54* *Playing Cards*. It had become a means of restoring to a composition a hint of realism; also a means of re-introducing colour, not for any descriptive purpose but in a way that was indepen-

49 *Homage to J. S. Bach* 1912

dent of images and unrelated to the distribution of light within a picture. Here, too, was a pictorial element that *appeared* to be real, and was in fact make-believe. To a painter who had already shown that he placed a high value on the incongruous, this little deception must have added an extra touch of pleasure.

The full usefulness of these simulated wood surfaces (marble surfaces were brought in later) as a means of re-introducing colour to Cubism did not emerge until later that year. Braque had rented a house during the latter part of the summer in the small town of Sorgues in the Rhône Valley near Avignon, where Picasso was also staying. (Braque, who had recently married, was to spend his summers here with his wife for the next fourteen years.) The two painters spent much of their time conducting experiments with cut-out paper and metal, designed

50 *Fruit-Dish and Glass* 1912
The first *papier collé*.

51 *Still-Life with a Bunch of Grapes* 1912 ▶

to bring colour back into their compositions: Picasso's survive but Braque's do not. Then in September Picasso left on a visit to Paris. In a spirit of inventive fun he had already, a few months previously, pasted to the middle of a picture, *Still-Life on a Chair,* a piece of actual oil-cloth printed to look like the cane-work seat of a chair. While Picasso was away Braque took this idea a stage further: he decided to try combining strips of coloured wallpaper, printed to simulate wood-panelling, not with a painting (as Picasso had done) but with a black and white charcoal drawing. In this way the coloured area was kept distinct, but at the same time the two separate elements could be combined within a single composition by extending the drawing *over* the pasted areas of wallpaper. The result was

Ill. 50   *Fruit-Dish and Glass,* the first *papier collé.*

On his return to Paris in October Braque showed this dis-covery to Picasso, who soon began to make use of it himself. The phase known as Synthetic Cubism had begun. Braque maintained that 'colour came into its own with *papiers collés.* . . .

74

With these works we succeeded in dissociating colour from form, in putting it on a footing independent of form, for that was the crux of the matter. Colour acts simultaneously with form, but has nothing to do with form.' 'From then on', he said on another occasion, 'all kinds of new developments became possible.'

One further development – to be of the profoundest value to Braque from the 1930s onwards – had already taken place during that remarkably fecund and crowded year, 1912. In his painting Braque always attached the deepest importance to materials and their plastic qualities; but hitherto he had remained content to exploit the natural properties of oil-paint. Whatever effects of tactility he sought had been achieved by the conventional use of sensitive brush-work. But in the spring and summer of 1912 Braque began to vary and enhance the tactile element in his work by mixing other materials with oil-paint – sand in particular and to a lesser extent ash, sawdust, even metal filings and tobacco. *Still-Life with a Bunch of Grapes,* painted on *Ill. 51*

75

a sand ground, is among the first of Braque's compositions to make extensive use of this technique. In 1954 the publication *Cahiers d'Art* printed what remains the most valuable of Braque's published statements, edited by Dora Vallier, in which the artist described in the following manner this moment in the evolution of his ideas.

'Speaking purely for myself', said Braque, 'I can say that it was my very acute feeling for the *matière,* for the substance of painting, which pushed me into thinking about the possibilities of the medium. I wanted to create a sort of substance by means of brush-work. But that is the kind of discovery which one makes gradually, though once a beginning has been made other discoveries follow. Thus it was that I subsequently began to introduce sand, sawdust and metal filings into my pictures. For I suddenly saw the extent to which colour is related to substance. If, for instance, two pieces of white material, each of a different texture, are dipped in the same dye, they will emerge a different colour. Now, this intimate relationship between colour and substance is inevitably even more delicate when it comes to painting. So my great delight was the "material" character which I could give to my pictures by introducing these extraneous elements. In short, they provided me with a means of getting further away from idealism in "representing" the things with which I was concerned.'

Where Analytical Cubism, particularly in its final 'Hermetic' phase, had grown intensely complicated and highly wrought, to the point of obscurantism, Synthetic Cubism tended the other way. Almost bland simplicity attends many of Braque's finest paintings and *papiers collés* of 1913 such as *Aria de Bach* and *The Cinema Programme.* All concern with analysis and definition of objects has receded. In *Aria de Bach* a pale remnant of Analytical Cubism lingers in the pencilled outline of a violin and some less specific lines in charcoal that softly mark the white paper; but they are no more than the frailest scaffolding to which three dark cut-out areas of colour are affixed. These areas are in no sense representational. They may suggest the

Ill. 52
Ill. 53

76

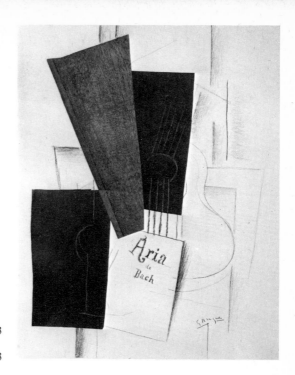

52 *Aria de Bach* 1913

53 *The Cinema Programme* 1913

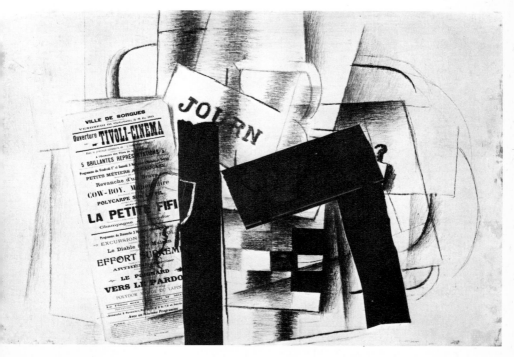

54 *Still-Life*
with Playing Cards 1913

materials of musical instruments but they certainly do not describe the instruments.

Similarly, in *The Cinema Programme,* the dark cut-out areas play no descriptive role whatever. The still-life theme is established by the feathery drawing which remains for the most part in the background except where it spills across the Tivoli-Cinéma poster and across the pasted cut-outs of textured paper. And in a more involved composition of the same year, *Still-Life* Ill. 54 *with Playing Cards,* the images (table, bunch of grapes, apple, cards, newspaper) are established by means of faint charcoal drawing in the Analytical manner. But with the exception of the red ace of hearts, texture and colour (in this case areas of simulated wood-texturing) have once again been kept separate, freed from any descriptive role.

78

Fundamentally, the shift from Analytical to Synthetic Cubism is a change not of subject but of approach to that subject. Previously the painter attempted a single coherent analysis of a group of objects, and of his experience of those objects. Now in place of the highly complicated analysis offered by Analytical Cubism, Braque has turned to an extremely simple analysis, but one in which different aspects of his theme – form, colour and substance – are treated separately. Description of actual form is now confined to the drawing, while colour and substance have been separated from form and contribute to the composition rather in the manner of a metaphor.

As in the final phase of Analytical Cubism in 1911, Braque in 1913 might appear to have reached once again a point that was only a single step from abstraction. He had liberated colour and substance from their descriptive role; and in doing so he had accepted (above all in the *papiers collés*) that the sensuous elements of a theme could be supplied by means of strips of coloured or textured material with no directly representational function. Inevitably such a course resulted in a body of work whose dominant features have nothing of visual reality about them whatever. Take away the faint passages of drawing from *Aria de Bach* and the result is an abstract composition pure and simple.

Ill. 52

But, as on earlier occasions, the crisis of imminent abstraction may seem more acute in retrospect than it did to the painters themselves in 1913. It is certain that Braque would never have created *Aria de Bach* without the seminal idea of a still-life composition incorporating a violin and a musical score. The 'abstract' areas, in other words, could never have taken over completely since their very existence depended upon, and was related to, a specific concrete image without which there would have been no painting.

That Braque was able to use the discovery of *papier collé* as a means of re-introducing colour to his favourite Cubist themes, is demonstrated in the painting *Woman with a Guitar* of 1913, and in still-life compositions such as *Glass and Violin* and

Ill. 26
Ill. 56

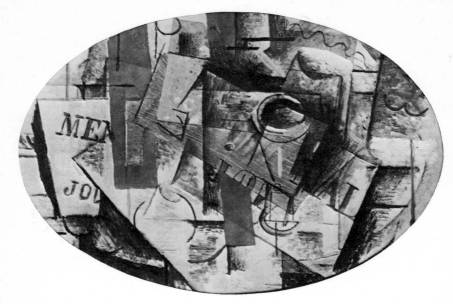

The Violin, both completed during the early part of 1914; while in *Music* and more particularly *The Bottle of Rum,* both painted later in 1914, Braque has grown so confident in his non-descriptive use of colour that he has begun to indulge in a playful affection for textures that are decorative and very little more. In *Music* heavily textured areas of gesso and sawdust contrast with soft passages of charcoal drawing, and with further areas that are spotted in a *pointilliste* manner: and in *The Bottle of Rum* this *pointilliste* decoration has spread across virtually the entire surface.

Ills. 57, 58

As if in reaction to the disciplines imposed upon his lyrical spirit during the past seven years, Braque has suddenly burst into flippant gaiety. These are the last bright sparks of his association with Picasso. War was about to break out and to cut three years out of his own career. The association never re-formed.

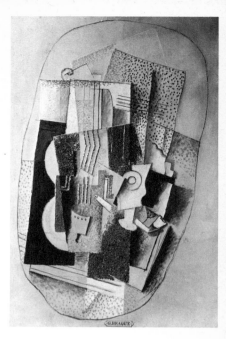

56 *Glass and Violin* 1913–14   57 *Music* 1914

CHAPTER SIX

The break

Braque received his call-up papers at Sorgues, where he had spent much of the previous two summers. In 1913 he had returned to Sorgues after a brief stay at Céret with Picasso and Gris, and in 1914 he was again joined there by Picasso, this time with Derain. It was Picasso (like Gris a Spanish national and therefore exempt from military service) who saw him off at Avignon Station. Braque, having already done a year's military training (in 1901–2), was promptly commissioned and sent to the Front, where he became that most expendable piece of military equipment, a First World War lieutenant in the infantry.

On 30 October Juan Gris wrote to Kahnweiler, self-exiled in Switzerland, 'I have no news of Braque, the person who interests me most' (Gris letters, edited and translated by Douglas Cooper). On 11 May 1915, after being twice mentioned in dispatches, Braque was almost killed by a wound in the head at Carency (Artois), and temporarily lost his sight. On 1 June Gris wrote to Kahnweiler, 'He has been seriously wounded but is now out of danger. Yesterday he was brought to a hospital here [*viz.* Paris]. I expect to see him tomorrow. He was hit in the head by shrapnel and he has been trepanned. . . . While he was on the danger list he kept it all quiet. He's a wonderful person. I have been terribly worried on his account because, as you know, I am very fond of him.'

Braque's convalescence was long and his recovery gradual. Almost nine months later Gris wrote, to Maurice Raynal, on 22 February 1916, 'Braque is under observation at the hospital at Evreux where his future will be decided.' He was sent off on sick-leave shortly afterwards and joined his wife at Sorgues: later in the year he was discharged from the army as unfit.

Braque returned to civilian life with the *Légion d'Honneur* and *Croix de Guerre* for his pains; and in January 1917 his close friends, including Juan Gris and the sculptor Henri Laurens, held a banquet in Paris in his honour. Back at Sorgues that summer Braque felt at last well enough to paint again. It was almost three years since he had left to join up.

The First World War left a scar on Braque but it left no noticeable scar on his work. From his earliest days human activity of any kind had never engaged him as a painter. Perhaps in the final analysis this is one of Braque's limitations. One may readily imagine what Picasso might have made of such an experience of the trenches, had it come his way; but for Braque there was nothing in the war but personal suffering, which he considered was irrelevant to his art. Braque's was a world of stillness, not action; of reflection, not engagement; of things, not people. Objects were his *dramatis personae*; people his scenery. Gris once shrewdly said of him, 'In the guitar Braque found his new Madonna.' The war thundered away outside the cell of Braque's creative life. In the end it did no more than break for a while the chain of development built up over the previous nine years; and it gave him time to reflect upon what he had achieved and upon the direction he should now take. Perhaps – and this can only be speculation – it was the experience of war that brought home to Braque how little of the panorama of life actually touched the artist in him and how far his true interests lay from the passions and affairs of mankind. Whether this occurred or not, certainly the post-war Braque seems a lonelier though more self-reliant painter, more introspective, more at terms with the strengths and the limitations of his own natural gifts.

It was during his long convalescence in hospital that he wrote, among a group of maxims later published in the review *Nord-Sud* in December 1917, 'In art progress consists not in extension but in the knowledge of its limits.' It is a remark of a man who knows his way, and who has also come to accept the narrowness of that way. The effect of the war, then, was not

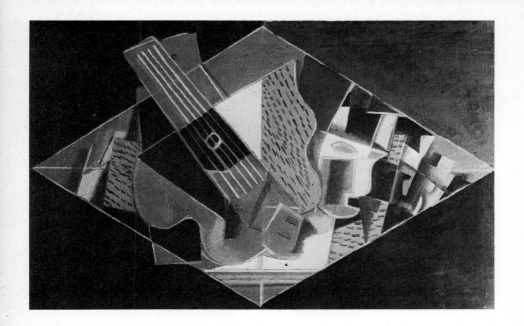

so much to alter Braque's art as to change its pace and its mood, to deepen the convictions upon which it rested and, by breaking the partnership with Picasso, to sharpen its individual personality. Many of Braque's pre-war paintings could almost have been by the hand of Picasso (and vice versa). From 1917 his work was to permit no such confusion.

For a while he was content to work closely along the lines pursued by Picasso and Gris during the previous three years – as if he were catching up on the time missed; except that now a mood at once darker yet more colourful has settled on his work.
Ill. 60 The large figure composition, *The Musician* of 1917–18, is superficially very close to Gris and to Picasso. Its bold areas of red, blue, green and yellow, and its decorative patches textured to simulate wood-graining and printed fabrics, demonstrate a confidence in the use of colour (colour dissociated from form, that is) which Braque had found in the last years before the war. Only the range of colours is now his own – acid-yellow, soft deep green of foliage, brown of old wood – and the background

84

59 *The Guitar* 1917

60 *The Musician*
1917–18

The first major
composition Braque
completed after
his return from the
First World War.

Ill. 62

Ills. 63, 67 to the picture is for the first time dark, just as it is in many other late works of Synthetic Cubism which follow: *Clarinet, Guitar and Fruit-dish* and *Still-Life on a Table*, both 1918; *Café-Bar*, 1919, and *Still-Life with a Guitar*, 1921. This dark background is something new and entirely personal.

Ill. 61 Braque was to become a master of black ('Black is very rich as a colour', he said), and to employ it with wonderful richness and subtlety. Its early use here, like a foil to set off a gem, has the two principal effects of emptying the painting of exterior light, and of suggesting that all light within the picture radiates from the colours themselves. The overall tone of each of these paintings is sombre; yet each seems to possess a glow of fire. A similar effect is achieved in the collage *Guitar and Clarinet* of 1918, a work of sublime simplicity reminiscent of the pre-war *papiers collés,* simply by toning the empty background down to a smooth warm grey.

The dark background, by supplying a kind of solid wall against which to set colours and forms, also gives Braque's work at this time something of the appearance of a sculptural relief; and this may have been his intention. He had formed what was to remain a lifelong friendship with the sculptor, Henri Laurens, whose own Cubist reliefs suggest a strong influence of Braque's ideas, and the impact may well have been reciprocal. Apart from a small plaster figure which he carved in a spirit of curiosity in 1920, Braque showed no inclination to make sculpture himself at this time; on the other hand his growing concern with the tactility of the paint surface was naturally guiding his interest in that direction. In this respect these post-war compositions of Braque, painted between 1917 and 1919, represent the climax of Synthetic Cubism, also the climax of the artist's quest to bring every area of a picture within reach. The black background virtually hurls each coloured shape into the spectator's face. Again one is reminded of Braque's remark on the appeal to him of the still-life, 'because in the still-life you have a tactile, I might almost say a manual space. . . . This answered to the hankering I have always had to touch things and not merely

86

see them. It was this space that particularly attracted me . . .'
(quoted by Leymarie).

Braque's reputation and artistic personality had until now
been overshadowed by that of his more eye-catching contemporaries. In his Fauvist years (1905–7) he was seen, rightly, to be a
follower of Matisse. In the Cubist years that followed he had
been widely considered, much less rightly, to be the Horatio to
Picasso's Hamlet. Before 1919 Braque's commercial and critical
success had been only moderate. But in that year Braque held a
one-man exhibition at the Paris gallery of his new dealer,
Léonce Rosenberg (Kahnweiler was still abroad), and this
gained him relatively high prices for the first time. In addition
it gained him a reputation as a painter who had made a striking
and original contribution to the – by now fashionable – Cubist
movement.

61 *Guitar and Clarinet* 1918
One of the most successful of the post-war *papiers collés.*

62 *Clarinet, Guitar and Fruit-dish* 1918

It was belated recognition for a pioneer of Cubism. But at least respect, when it did come Braque's way, was paid to some of the most triumphantly beautiful canvases of his career. These included a number of the compositions on black-primed canvas, among them *Still-Life on a Table* now in Philadelphia, which is an early example of Braque's favourite theme of the *guéridon* or upright table, and the oval *Clarinet, Guitar and Fruit-dish*. Like *The Black Guéridon,* done in 1919, these paintings show Braque developing a more relaxed, more sensuous, less calculated treatment of colours and forms. The stiff geometry of *The Musician,* painted only a few months earlier, has loosened;

Ill. 62
Ill. 64

Ill. 60

shapes have grown supple; outlines are sometimes sharp as wire, sometimes soft as clouds. A sensitivity to the luxuriant richness of paint as a substance – white semi-transparent over black, green emerging out of grey, one simulated texture contrasted with another, a rough texture with a smooth – is now the lodestar of his imagination. One senses in this group of paintings that Braque is no longer actively engaged in solving compositional problems; that he has thoroughly absorbed the lessons of Cubism and now feels free to shed its disciplines and allow his own lyrical talents to take command.

These are transitional paintings. They are still recognizably in the Cubist idiom, but already they look forward to the major set-pieces of the 1920s. In *Café-Bar,* for instance, the simple *Ill. 63* division of both the table-leg and the musical instrument into a light area and a dark area foreshadows what was to become throughout the '20s and '30s Braque's characteristic method of describing a three-dimensional object. His colour range – black and white, ochre and olive-green, sky-blue, rust-red, acid-yellow and a heavy outlining of objects in black – likewise anticipates the work of the '20s. The delicate clusters of fruit hint at the numerous small 'cabinet-pictures' (the *sine qua non* of countless well-bred American households between the wars) which Braque was soon to paint as exercises in pure craftsmanship between larger and more taxing compositions. And the arrangement of objects on a circular table in *The Black Guéridon,* and the suggestion of wall-panelling that occurs in the same painting, introduce a theme that was to obsess Braque for more than a quarter of a century to come: how to group objects together and present them, not just by themselves isolated from their natural surroundings (as in the 'cabinet-paintings'), but as the focal point in the enclosed space of a room.

Having mastered, during the Cubist years, how to bring every object forward to the picture surface and how to express space and volume without recourse to the illusion of perspective, Braque began to 'rediscover' space, first – in the '20s and '30s – to bring within reach and within touch the four walls of

64 *The Black Guéridon* 1919

a room; then in the great *Studio* series of the late '40s and '50s to suggest that those four walls were no longer entirely substantial but were also avenues leading to spaces beyond; and finally towards the end of his life to reach even further and embrace the whole sky and horizon.

◀ 63 *Café-Bar* 1919

Digression I: Space and Reality

Braque drew much of his inspiration from *objects* – from simple everyday objects around him: fruit, musical instruments, furniture, bottles and so on. *Réalité* was an important and recurrent word in his vocabulary, and he strove for much of his career to attain it. But what exactly did he mean by *réalité*? It is immediately obvious that he recognized a profound difference between the reality of an actual apple in a three-dimensional surrounding, and that of an apple represented by a two-dimensional image on the picture surface. The latter was not a straightforward account of the former: neither was it intended to evoke in the spectator's mind a real apple by offering the illusion of a three-dimensional object, which had been the fixed tradition of still-life painting from De Heem to Cézanne.

The special character of Braque's compositions stems from the artist's rejection of this traditional relationship between actual and painted object. The painted image of an apple is of course bound to an *idea* of a real apple – Braque always made that quite clear – but it was never supposed to *represent* a real apple. Its reality lay in the fact that it was a painted apple, not a painting of an apple. This meant that the apple not only had to be interpreted according to the artist's experience, and in terms of paint as a material; it also had to be interpreted two-dimensionally. Merely to have produced a flat version of a three-dimensional image, as a camera will do, was to Braque a kind of lie. It missed the point of what painting was about by offering the mere illusion of reality, instead of arriving at a different kind of reality.

This view of the nature and role of painting, and of its relationship to life itself, was formulated during the early days of Cubism with Picasso: but to all intents and purposes it remained Braque's view long after he had abandoned Cubism. Braque held that the Renaissance tradition of painting in perspective, which aimed at supplying the illusion of a third dimension, was a false one from which, at the moment of his discovery of Cézanne in 1907, he began to plot a systematic withdrawal.

This retreat from what he felt to be the entirely wrong course taken by European painters since the fifteenth century, demanded courage and abundant self-confidence. (In his later years Braque even refused to visit museums to *look at* the Old Masters.) The dangers of getting lost were great indeed. Hence perhaps the strict limitation Braque imposed on his range of subject-matter, and the procedures – sometimes clumsy procedures – he was compelled to adopt in order to avoid creating any illusion of perspective whatever. Hence, too, Braque's early abandonment of the practice of working directly from life; and his fondness for the kind of deliberate ambiguity (this is something I return to in a later Digression) which successfully disperses all attempts at a literal interpretation of his work.

All the same, little of Braque's art is experimental, and in this he differs widely from Picasso for whom experiment is woven into the fabric of all he touches. The art of Georges Braque is systematic and logical. It is formal to its very roots, while remaining deeply personal and private. It is rarely showy, never passionate. People do not count for much, and when they feature at all it is as formal objects. Correspondingly his development as a painter proceeds along largely formal lines. Innovations of colour, materials and imagery perform a role curiously dispassionate for one whose art is so intimate. The violin, the basket of fruit, the lamp, the billiard-table: that such images are steeped in personal meaning there can be no question, yet their primary role in Braque's work remains a formal one. That is to say, they assist in that methodical series of restatements concerning the experience of space of which the body of Braque's work consists; they are the furniture in that space, they give it reality, humanize it, they are the entirely familiar things which inhabit and make that space his own.

Consider in outline that series of restatements. As a Fauvist Braque remained content, like the others, with a simplified form of conventional perspective. He merely adopted the practice which had already been pursued by Matisse and Derain of raising the angle of view so that a landscape became

foreshortened and appeared to slope towards the spectator. *Hills*
Ill. 14 *at La Ciotat* of 1907 is characteristic of these foreshortened
'tumbling' landscapes. In his Cézannian paintings of the
Ill. 12 following year, such as *Landscape at L'Estaque*, Braque has now
adopted a geometrical approach to landscape, slicing it into
defined planes as if it were built up of playing-cards, and
bringing the whole scene closer to the eye by blocking out
sky and horizon altogether. Otherwise the vertical 'tumbling'
format remains as before; and it persists in many of the finest
works of Analytical Cubism, such as the Solomon Guggenheim
Ill. 37 Museum's superb *Piano and Lute* of 1910, and the equally fine
Ill. 44 *Woman Reading* painted during the so-called 'Hermetic' phase
of Cubism a year later.

In these two last pictures the scene has merely shifted from
landscape to still-life, and the volume of space suggested by
each picture has accordingly been reduced to a minimum. It
is in this context that Braque's often-made comment acquires
its point: 'In tactile space you measure the distance separating
you from the object, whereas in visual space you measure the
distance separating things from each other. This is what led me,
long ago, from landscape to still-life.'

By the time we advance to Synthetic Cubism Braque's
compositions have been emptied of a sense of space altogether.
Ill. 52 *Aria de Bach* of 1913 is quite flat. Thereafter, since clearly no
further advance could be made in this direction, something of
the reverse process begins to operate. In the later Synthetic
Ill. 60 Cubist pictures, such as *The Musician* of 1917–18, a certain
sense of volume within the painting has returned, but this is
now supplied by a careful balance of dominant and recessive
colours, and not by any illusion of a third dimension.

Then in the 1920s, part of the interior space of an actual room
Ill. 68 begins to find its way back into canvases like *The Mantelpiece*
Ill. 89 of 1921 and, in a more pronounced manner, *The Guéridon* of
1928–9. By the 1940s and early 1950s this space has expanded
to such an extent that the entire volume of a room is suggested,
Ill. 119 in for instance *The Billiard-Table* of 1944–52 and, more subtly,

94

Studio VIII of 1955; while in the final phase of Braque's work *Ill. 147* the pendulum has swung back so far that the very aspects of space which Braque first sought to eliminate from his work – sky and horizon – have become the principal themes of paintings such as *Boats on the Beach* (1949) and *On the Wing* *Ills. 123, 156* (1956–61).

In the late landscapes the paint is thickly encrusted. The sky looks as heavy as a rough-stone wall, with layer upon layer of paint, thin over thick, accumulating the maximum effect of tactility and in the process dispelling any possible illusion of real space, of real sky. Once again reality for Braque is first of all the reality of a painted surface, out of which an image may have emerged almost as an afterthought. *On the Wing* is a case in point: the lower-left section, enclosing a second bird in flight, was lightly painted over a crusty area of sky five years after the picture had been exhibited as complete at both the Edinburgh Festival and Tate Gallery.

'Compelled by the desire to go further towards an expression of space, I wanted to avail myself of the faculty of touch', Braque recounted to Dora Vallier in the important series of statements published in *Cahiers d'Art* in October 1954. '. . . it was my very acute feeling for the *matière* . . . which pushed me into thinking about the possibilities of the medium. . . . Thus it was that I subsequently began to introduce sand, sawdust and metal filings into my pictures. . . .' And the more Braque grew to convey the reality of painted forms by such tactile means, the more he strove to dissuade the spectator from identifying those painted forms too literally with the images they seemed to represent in life.

On one page of the *Cahier* which he compiled during a serious illness in the 1940s Braque wrote the three words '*Imprégnation – Obsession – Hallucination*'. Braque, the man who talked so often of *réalité,* and whose art was so firmly rooted in the love of plain domestic objects, yet grew to possess an almost mystical faith in the imponderable. 'Reality is not imitation, but magic', he wrote in a statement published by Christian

Zervos in *Cahiers d'Art No. 10, 1935*. Dora Vallier records another *bon mot*:'It is important not to imitate what one wishes to create.' A more celebrated quip, from Braque's own *Cahier* (published in 1948), reads 'The function of Art is to disturb. Science reassures.' Or again from the *Cahier*: 'Whatever is in common is true; but likeness is false. Trouillebert's work bears a likeness to that of Corot, but they have nothing in common.'

In effect when Braque spoke of the importance of *réalité* he meant two separate things. He meant the dependence of art upon the physical world we live in. And he meant, besides, that it was important to recognize the extent to which art acquires a different and autonomous reality from that of life itself. Braque believed in what he frequently called a 'poetic' view of things. 'The only valid thing in art is that which cannot be explained', he recounted to John Richardson (*The Observer*, 1 December 1957). 'To explain away the mystery of a great painting – if such a feat were possible – would be irreparable harm. . . . Mysteries have to be respected if they are to retain any power. . . . If there is no mystery then there is no "poetry", the quality I value above all else in art. What do I mean by "poetry"? It is to a painting what life is to man. . . . For me it is a matter of harmony, of *rapports*, of rhythm and – most important for my own work – of "metamorphosis".' And of metamorphosis more in a later Digression.

CHAPTER SEVEN

The solemn '20s

In the Cubist years when Braque and Picasso had felt themselves to be 'like two mountaineers roped together', they had pursued a narrow and disciplined course for fear of losing the way. The work of the two painters never became impersonal but it did grow almost indistinguishable, as each sought to eliminate from his work the fingerprints of individual personality. They pursued their course in the manner of explorers, and explorers have to subordinate their own temperament to the task in hand. From the work of the pre-war and immediately post-war years it is perfectly feasible to pin-point and measure the progress of both artists, as if making a chart of their ascent. But having reached a kind of summit, a point from which no further systematic progress was possible, Picasso and Braque went their diverse ways. Braque's own path not only levelled out, it broadened and split into several ways that ran more or less parallel.

From the early '20s several themes occupied his mind concurrently. He also liked to work on different scales, and at a varying pitch of intensity. He began what was to become a life-time practice of having in his studio a number of half-finished canvases at any one time (towards the end of his life there might be as many as thirty of these, some waiting more than ten years for the final touch). Altogether Braque's development grew less chronologically consistent. It was also a time of applied craftsmanship, when his energies were concentrated on using the textures of paint and the harmonies of colour to enrich the sensuous properties of still-life objects.

One of the several paths he pursued during the '20s was the theme of the still-life raised on an upright table or mantelpiece, and presented in a tall vertical format. *The Mantelpiece* is the   *Ill. 68*

◀   65 *Woman with a Mandolin* 1917

66 *Anemones* 1924

first of four versions painted between 1921 and 1927, and closely related to them are a number of other upright com-

Ill. 73 positions such as *Still-Life with Guitar and Fruit* of 1924, *The*
Ill. 83 *Marble Table* of 1925, and several new versions of his favourite
Ills. 79, 89, *Guéridon* theme painted in 1928 and 1929. In these paintings
91 Braque achieved a powerful effect of monumentality by piling the still-life objects into the upper or central area of the canvas, and supporting them upon the massive upright forms of a table or mantelpiece as if they were raised upon Classical columns. Extensive use of marble-texturing further enhanced this dignified effect, while in *Still-Life with Guitar and Fruit* the drapery that hangs down over the side of the table has been folded in such a way as to hint at the fluting of a column.

In 1922, a year when the Salon d'Automne honoured the artist's fortieth birthday with a room of eighteen of his paintings,

67 *Still-Life with Guitar* 1921

Braque started to explore a subject even more markedly Classical than the large upright still-lifes, that of the *Canephori* (or *Ceremonial Basket Bearers*). It is very likely that the hefty female nudes of Picasso's own 'Classical' period (begun in 1919) suggested to Braque the possibilities of treating such a theme, very much as Picasso's *Demoiselles d'Avignon* had inspired the large *Nude* of 1907–8; only this time Braque's response was not imitative, if response it was. The massive slump of the bodies of these basket bearers, the graceful turn of a head, the formal arrangement of each figure against a flat and often marble-textured background, and the almost impersonal way the brush has traced the heavy folds of flesh: these are not qualities which derive in any way from Picasso.

Rather, the *Canephori* are Braque's tribute to Ingres and Corot, and to Renoir. They have, besides, a natural affinity with

Ills. 71, 72

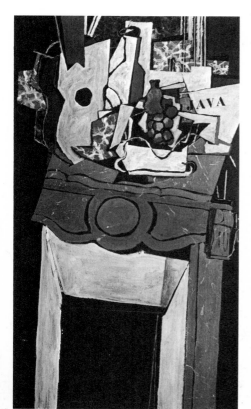

68 *The Mantelpiece* 1921

From the 1920s Braque became increasingly fond of painting variations on a single theme. That of the mantelpiece, with still-life objects crowded upon it, was one of the first he explored in his immediately post-Cubist days.

69 JEAN-BAPTISTE
CAMILLE COROT
Portrait of
Christine Nilsson
1874

Braque had
a reproduction of
Corot's painting on
the wall of his studio.
He acknowledged his
debt to the great
nineteenth-century
Frenchman in a
figure-study (far right).
After Cézanne and
Picasso, Corot was the
artist who influenced
Braque most profoundly
all his life.

his own *Mantelpiece* and *Guéridon* still-lifes of the same period. This is particularly true of the earliest pair of *Canephori*, painted in 1922–3, in which statuesque figures bear baskets of fruit above their heads in the manner of caryatids. There is a natural link here with Braque's upright tables and mantelpieces which likewise manage to suggest Classical architecture, and likewise support a basket of fruit or a bowl of flowers. Nor is this the only comparison. Caryatids, tables, mantelpieces: all three fulfil the role in Braque's pictures of raising the horizontal plane (represented in each case by a still-life) to the upper part of the picture, so compelling the eye to follow a vertical line upwards, only to look down on the basket of fruit, or guitar and bottle, held there. This double viewpoint, in which the spectator is made to look *up* at the lower part of a picture and down at the higher part, was always a favourite device of Braque's for disorientating the viewer.

102

70 *Souvenir de Corot* 1922–3

71 *Canephorus* 1922–3

72 *Canephorus* 1922–3

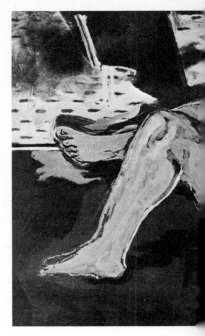

75 *Reclining Nude* 1924

73 *Still-Life with Guitar and Fruit* 1924

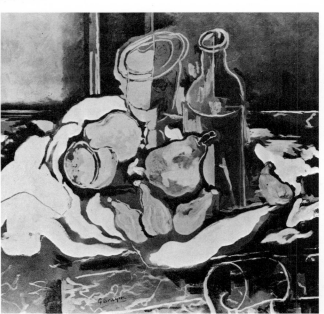

A curious affinity links Braque's reclining nudes of the 1920s with the still-lifes of the same period. The artist looked for forms common to both. His nudes tend to be impersonal, his still-lifes sensuous.

The figure subjects that follow the first pair of *Canephori* are altogether softer and more sensuous in treatment. In them the link with Renoir emerges more clearly. Some are reclining nudes; others take the form of bathers; in another, drawn in response to a commission from Diaghilev to design the décor for Kochno's ballet *Les Fâcheux* based on Molière, the figure reclines in a shell and bears an olive-branch in one hand; while still others are seated figures bearing a basket of fruit on their knees rather as if they were preciously holding one of Braque's own small cabinet-paintings. So often it is this luscious detail of fruit which is the focal point of these pictures. However impressive and monumental the figures themselves, they remain attendant rather than central figures; and they fulfil a ceremonial function which is to present, and draw attention to, a still-life.

76 *Reclining Nude* 1925

106

77 *Nude with Basket of Fruit* 1925

The mid-1920s were rich in small still-lifes. These cabinet-paintings, which manage to combine so effortlessly the French *nature morte* tradition with a new pictorial language developed from Cubism, are in some respects the very quintessence of Braque. Small in scale, humble in theme, exuding an unaffected relish for the pleasures of plain bourgeois living, they are like interval music played as a relaxation between more demanding tasks. They are the purest examples of Braque the craftsman, and of Braque the lover of things simple and everyday. They are also Braque's point of closest contact with that earlier master of intimate still-life, Chardin, and through him with the Dutch seventeenth-century still-lifes that were so popular with the French in Chardin's day, and about which the term 'cabinet-pictures' was first used. A vase of flowers, a bowl of fruit, a pitcher and a bottle of wine, sometimes with the accompaniment of a guitar: Braque's theme is the table laden with all that invites a man to touch, smell, drink, eat and play. It is not altogether facetious to suggest that Braque's cabinet-pictures could only have been produced in a country renowned for its *cuisine*.

78 *Bather* 1925

79 *The Guéridon c.* 1928

80 *Mandolin, Glass, Pot and Fruit* 1927

81 *The Bottle of Marc* 1930

Braque's cabinet-pictures are the paintings of a man richly contented with his life. He was by now highly successful. All the eighteen major works he had exhibited at the 1922 Salon d'Automne had sold. Shortly before, he had been so incensed by his ex-dealer, Léonce Rosenberg, for grossly undervaluing Kahnweiler's stock of Cubist paintings (confiscated as the property of a German and put up for sale in the Hôtel Drouot) that he had struck him to the ground in public. In 1923 Braque received his commission from Diaghilev to design the décor for *Les Fâcheux*, with music by Georges Auric (two years later he was to receive a similar commission for Kochno's *Zéphyre et Flore*, also based on Molière). In 1924 he held another successful exhibition with his new dealer Paul Rosenberg, and later in the same year Braque moved from Montparnasse to a house built specially for him by the architect Auguste Perret in a quietly respectable street just off the Parc Montsouris. This was to remain his Paris home until he died.

Braque's small, relaxed still-lifes of the 1920s concern themselves with little more ambitious than a simplified interpretation of a range of flowers, fruit and domestic objects. Invariably these are expressed with the maximum attention to the volume of each object and to the sensuous tactile properties

Ills. 74, 83
Ills. 84, 66

of colour. *Bottle, Glass and Fruit* (1924), *The Marble Table* (1925), *Still-Life with Fruit* (1926) and *Anemones* (1924), are characteristic examples. Often, as in *The Marble Table,* he exploited the use of ornamental textured surfaces, employing to sumptuous effect the contrast of black and white areas thickly painted.

Ill. 85

Ill. 87

In 1927 Braque completed a number of still-lifes in which black plays as important a role as it had in the late Cubist pictures of 1917–19. *The Black Rose,* painted about 1927, is sharply divided between dark and light areas, with the rose itself in silhouette, while in *Guitar, Fruit and Pitcher,* 1927, Braque has thickly outlined each key image in black, a practice followed by Cézanne in a number of his still-life compositions of the late 1870s and 1880s.

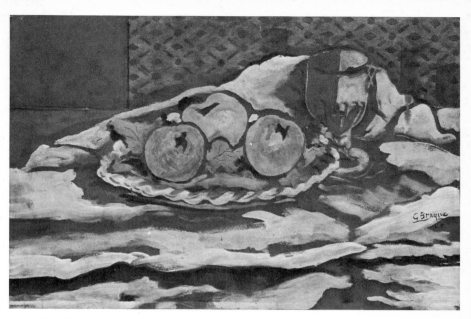

82 *Still–Life* 1925

83 *The Marble Table* 1925

Braque's love of
decorative surfaces
became a dominant
feature of his paintings
from the mid–1920s until
the late 1930s. The
marbling effect used here
was another of the skills
the artist had acquired
while training for his
father's profession of
house–painter.

84 *Still-Life with Fruit* 1926

86 *Table, Fruit and Jug* 1926 ▶

87 *Guitar, Fruit and Pitcher* 1927 ▶

85 *The Black Rose* 1927

88 *Head I* 1928

A simple geometrical
division into areas of light
and shadow became
another post-Cubist
stylistic device.

In a number of these paintings of the late '20s there are signs
that Braque's still-lifes are growing formularized and over-
emphatic, at the expense of those qualities of subtlety and
lyricism which had been characteristic of his major work
hitherto. Gone too is that perfectly timed note of incongruity
which had been the life-spark of so much of his best work. For
the first time an air of mass-production has settled on his work.
Again Braque was able to demonstrate a rare genius – a genius
that he was always able to call on when the way seemed blocked
– for discovering a fresh vitality and a new field of ideas within
the same range of themes that only a little time before had
seemed to be exhausted. (Ben Nicholson and Henry Moore are
two other twentieth-century artists blessed with a similar gift.)

In the still-lifes after 1927 just such a transformation took
place. In 1928 Braque abandoned the practice of priming

89 *The Guéridon* 1928–9

90 *The Large Table* 1929

91 *The Guéridon* (detail) 1928–9

118

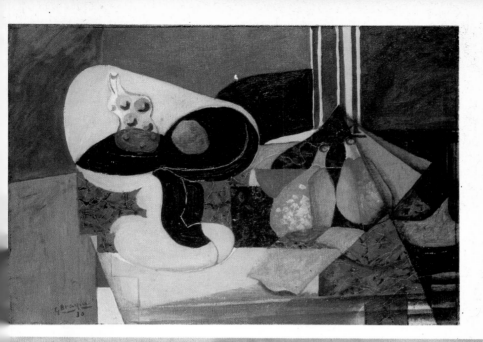

canvases with the dense black he had favoured for much of the previous decade. Instead, on a neutral priming, given a roughish texture with the aid of sand and gesso, he began to apply a bright mosaic of colours to a series of new variations on his favourite theme of the pedestal-table (or *guéridon*) with still-life objects grouped upon it. The familiar sharp division of these objects into light and dark areas remains prominent, but in pictures *Ill. 89* such as *The Guéridon* of 1928–9, and a related work *The Large* *Ill. 90* *Table* of 1929 – which show Braque's fondness for repeating certain images more or less exactly – these divisions between light and shade are now accompanied by sharply divided areas of colour, chiefly red, green, blue and yellow.

In most of this *Guéridon* series, and in other paintings related *Ill. 95* to it such as *The Blue Mandolin* of 1930, these coloured areas create a pattern of upright forms standing behind the table against the wall of the room in the manner of screens. The divisions between these 'screens' is frequently marked by an illusionistic shadow, as if Braque felt it important to emphasize the fact that distance lay between them. At the same time Braque began trying to convey a sense of the volume of the room itself by employing another illusionistic device (one that in his Cubist days he would have rejected totally), of suggesting that part of the wall-panelling recedes in perspective down one *Ill. 89* wall *(e.g., The Guéridon)*. Neither innovation appears strikingly effective. Both introduce a sense of a third dimension strikingly at odds with the flatness of the central group of images on the table. But they proclaim a new concern to surround a still-life composition with the sensation of space. This question of space contained within a canvas was to occupy Braque in a great many of the still-lifes painted during the 1930s, although it was not until a good many years later – in the *Billiard-Table* and *Studio* series in particular – that Braque was to discover a satisfactory way of achieving this effect without resorting to illusionistic devices.

CHAPTER EIGHT

Tracing his roots

For the first time since 1905 Braque spent part of the summer of 1929 on the Normandy coast where he had been brought up and had lived as a young man. Braque had given up his Provençal house at Sorgues after 1926, and had spent the next two summers at various places in the south including La Ciotat, where he had painted some of his finest Fauve pictures back in 1907. His return to Normandy was propitious, for it signalled a renewal of interest in landscape (he had not tackled a landscape since Céret in 1911), and a new receptivity to the light and colour of the countryside, banished from his paintings since the early Cubist days.

The moist silvery light of the Normandy coast, its cliffs, broad beaches and clear horizons which had meant so much to Boudin and Monet, now began to exert their appeal on Braque – tinged doubtless with a certain nostalgia. In 1931 he moved into a house specially designed and built for him in traditional Norman style at Varengeville, near Dieppe, and it was here that Braque spent much of the remainder of his life. But already on his first return visit to Dieppe in 1929 he had begun what was to become an infrequent series of small beach scenes (*Boats on the Beach, Dieppe* is among the earliest) spread over the remaining decades of his life. *Ill. 94*

Braque never considered himself to be a serious landscape painter, and he is supposed to have regarded these compositions (other examples are *Blue Boats* of 1937, *Cliffs* of 1938 and *Boats on the Beach* of 1949) as restful exercises between more demanding work, and for this reason writers on Braque have obediently belittled them. This does them injustice. Apart from being among the most attractive paintings in Braque's output, these beach paintings achieve for the first time a reconciliation *Ills. 106, 107* *Ill. 123*

94 *Boats on the Beach, Dieppe* 1929

between the imagery of still-life and the imagery of landscape. More important than this they achieve a reconciliation between *local* colour (descriptive of local atmosphere), which Braque had rejected since his Cézannian days, and *applied* colour (independent of a descriptive function), which he had favoured ever since. Thus the *répertoire* of forms used in the beach paintings – normally restricted to a group of boats on the sand set in front of a screen of vertically-divided cliffs – is a counterpart to the cluster of still-life objects on a table set in front of coloured screens, which characterize the *Guéridon* series of still-lifes done at much the same time (the two boats in *Ill. 94* even look like still-life objects grouped on a circular dish). The range of dusky colours, too, enlivened by a patch of lemon-yellow on the boats here and there, is similar to that of a great many small

122

95 *The Blue Mandolin (The Blue Guitar)* 1930

96 *The Grey Table* 1930

cabinet-pictures Braque painted during the 1920s. Furthermore, the sandy cliffs and shore are suggested by means of a dotted *pointilliste* surface which performs an attractive decorative role similar to that performed by the skilfully textured surfaces made to simulate wood and marble, which are a prominent feature of the still-lifes.

The beach scenes are the first of Braque's paintings in which the artist was able to employ the pictorial language he had developed to convey a sense of space that lies *beyond* the reach of a man's hand. They are also the first of Braque's paintings since before Cubism to include what was later to become of the profoundest spiritual importance to Braque: the sky.

In general Braque's paintings of the late '20s and early '30s grow increasingly linear and wiry. Human forms had begun to concern him again, and he completed a group of rather expressionless heads, sharply divided into a dark and light area or profile, with the features lightly drawn in with the brush in *Ill. 88* a manner that echoes Picasso (*e.g., Head I* of 1928). Less successful are a series of highly distorted *Bathers* (1929–31) which again suggest that Braque has had Picasso's recent work in mind, in this case the latter's beach scenes painted at Dinard in 1928. The curving rhythmic line so prominent in these two themes also features strongly in a group of uncharacteristic still-lifes which Braque painted in the early '30s (*e.g. Ill. 92*), with the familiar images of guitar, fruit and bottle loosely outlined in white or black, and wobbly-looking shapes reminiscent of Arp painted in light washes of colour forming a rhythmic pattern independent of the still-life itself.

Braque's preoccupation with line rather than mass during this period led him to one of his most striking innovations, the technique of drawing finely scratched lines on panels of plaster which he first covered with a dark paint (generally black), so that a thread of white, or patches of white, could be made to show through the dark surface. Braque obtained the idea for these *plâtres gravés* from pre-Classical Greek intaglios and (conceivably) from Greek vase painting and engraved Etruscan

124

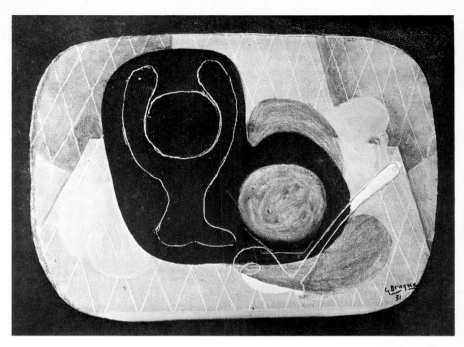

97 *The Clay Pipe* 1931

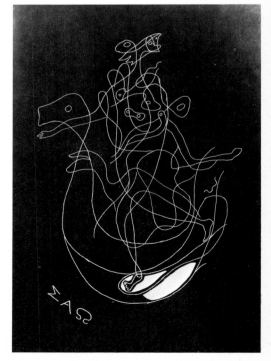

98 *A Nereid* 1931–2

mirrors, all of which are likely to have been familiar to him from the Louvre. Braque possessed in any case a profound love of Greek art, as the *Canephori* series had already suggested, and now the employment of a Classical (or pre-Classical) technique also awakened in him an interest in Classical themes and *Ill. 98* Classical heroes: *Herakles, Io, A Nereid* and so on. It was a result of working on the *plâtres gravés* that the dealer Ambroise Vollard commissioned from him sixteen etchings to illustrate an edition of Hesiod's *Theogony*. This heralded a period of varied graphic work that was to continue until the mid-'30s.

In 1932, the year in which he completed the sixteen Hesiod etchings, Braque was fifty. In the following year appeared Carl Einstein's admirable monograph on the artist, and the Kunsthalle in Basle awarded Braque his first major retrospective exhibition. It was appropriate that the Swiss, who were among the earliest and most perceptive collectors of Braque – hence the Swiss museums today are exceptionally rich in his work – should be the ones to bestow this honour on him. (A more dismal antithesis to the enthusiasm of the Swiss could scarcely have been found than the lukewarm reception which the British accorded Braque's first one-man exhibition in London a year later when, with prices at £55 upwards, a mere four pictures were sold at the Reid and Lefevre Gallery.)

DIGRESSION 2: REVOLUTION AND TRADITION
From his own writings Braque emerges as a man self-assured to the point of complacency. Yet towards his own art he adopted an attitude of the profoundest humility uncharacteristic of twentieth-century masters. 'I do not do what I want, I do what I can', he wrote in his *Cahier*. Braque accepted limitations and worked strictly within them, strove to make a virtue of them. His art is disciplined, muted, it is an art of understatement, without shocks. His paintings may be radical and often extreme statements, but they possess none of the restlessness or instability of the age. There is little of the intuitive guesswork and sense of risk that have landmarked the

career of Picasso. There are few of the swaggering gestures of trespass into the territory of unreason and disorder which at times seized Ernst and Kandinsky. There is no daringly original concept of colour, such as Matisse evolved. There is none of the uncompromising extremism of Malevich and Mondrian.

Braque manages to appear something of an *éminence grise* amid the upheavals of twentieth-century art. Already in his lifetime he had acquired something of the status of an Old Master, a figure of impeccable seriousness of purpose and grandeur, an artist who appeared to stand in honourable line of descent in French painting from Chardin to Corot to Cézanne: in short, a painter who – when his achievements were assessed together – may be said to have looked back rather than forwards.

How much of a revolutionary, then, was Braque? And to what extent did he settle down to being something else after his return from the First World War and his break with Picasso? There can be no question but that the rebel who astonished Paris with the first Cubist exhibition ever held, in 1908, mellowed into a kind of independent conservative in his later years. 'I am not a revolutionary painter', he maintained unequivocally in his *Cahier* of 1948. Talking to Dora Vallier some years later Braque made a similar claim for his Cubist paintings, adding by way of an explanation that Cubism was not 'directed against any other kind of painting' (*Cahiers d'Art*, October 1954).

His own view of his role tended to alter with mood as well as with age. 'I always felt a loathing of official painting', he also told Dora Vallier, 'and I have retained this intensely ever since.' These are scarcely the words of a reactionary old academician. His scorn for mere imitators was no less bitter, and his *Cahier* includes a characteristically sardonic comment: 'People who take the lead have their backs to those who follow. And that is exactly what those who follow deserve.'

Of course where Braque shows himself to be most revolutionary is in his Cubist treatment of form and space. The strength of the artist's feelings is expressed in a comment reported by John Richardson (part of it is quoted elsewhere in this book): 'The whole Renaissance tradition is antipathetic to me. The hard-and-fast rules of perspective which it succeeded in imposing on art were a ghastly mistake, which it has taken four centuries to redress; Cézanne and after him Picasso and myself can take a lot of credit for this. . . . Scientific perspective . . . forces the objects in a picture to disappear away from the beholder instead of bringing them within his reach as painting should.'

Cézanne had remained content to express his ideas within the conventions of geometrical perspective. But Braque, like Picasso, saw perspective only as a deception and a lie. Cézanne, in achieving his effect of a multiple viewpoint, bent orthodoxy to fix his purpose: Braque and Picasso attacked it. In doing so they were drawn to attack, too, the conventions and ideals of pictorial realism which had remained unchallenged since the Renaissance; for with the rejection of perspective – of the illusion of a third dimension – came inevitably the next step: an object was denied a literal and naturalistic representation. Images became, instead, 'diagrams' of that object, consisting of a description of it from all angles simultaneously, and this 'diagram' had to be sorted out in the mind of the spectator before he could create for himself any naturalistic impression of the object. Cubism invited the intellect to participate in the experience of reality.

Braque's Cubist years were rich in innovations. A great many of these were of course shared with Picasso, yet they leave no doubt in the mind that during those years the French painter was working out ideas with extraordinary daring and inventiveness, and with little or no respect for the accepted traditions upon which contemporary painting rested. After his key role in the early stages of Cubism, Braque continued to contribute a full share of ideas to its later developments in the years immediately before the First World War. He was the first to introduce lettering in a composition (1910): his were the first *papiers collés* and the first simulated marble-and-wood textures (all 1912). During the same period it was his fascination for the tactility of materials, and his determination to free colour from form, that led Braque to become the first artist to explore the sensuous possibilities of mixing oil-paint with unconventional substances – sand, sawdust, ashes, tobacco, metal filings and so on.

Yet the innovator, the rebel, in Braque remained in essence a Classicist. 'The Wild Men of Paris' whom the American journalist Gelett Burgess was interviewing in 1908–9 for *The Architectural Record* were so far from 'wild' as to be on the verge of creating some of the most meticulously organized pictures in the whole of twentieth-century art – paintings like Picasso's *Portrait of D. H. Kahnweiler* and Braque's *The Mandolin,* both 1910. Paradoxically Cubism, for all its declared revolt against the canons of pictorial illusionism, remains the only art movement of this century that belongs to the humanist tradition to which the Italian Renaissance gave birth. It is also the supreme example in modern art of another Renaissance characteristic: the quest for a pictorial language that could embrace reason and order. A composition like Braque's *Aria de Bach* is as Classical *Ill. 52* as the composer whose name is inscribed upon it.

Braque's Classicism persisted long after he drifted from Cubism in the early '20s, but it expressed itself differently. With his loss of interest in Cubism and the corresponding softening of his vision, the emphasis on strict order and a tight composition grew less pronounced. Accompanying this trend towards looser compositions came a tendency – it was only a spasmodic tendency but it persisted to the end of his life – to evoke images and *personnages* taken from the art of Classical and Archaic Greece. The first such allusion is the series of *Canephori* (or *Ceremonial Basket Bearers*) which Braque began in 1922. About the last of these allusions is *Ajax* of 1955. Greek vase- *Ill. 148* painting became another persistent influence, especially in the 1930s and 1940s. Numerous paintings of this period include 'double-image' figures sharply divided into a light-coloured full-face described in a contemporary manner, and a dark

profile resembling impersonalized figures taken from the side
Ill. 104 of an Attic vase. *Woman with an Easel* of 1936 is a particularly good demonstration of fondness for combining antique and modern in this manner.

In a similar way, when in 1931 he undertook a series of etchings to illustrate Hesiod's *Theogony* (a book which made a profound impression on the artist), Braque developed a wiry linear manner of representing figures that was strongly suggestive of pre-Classical Greek intaglios and of Etruscan mirror-engravings, both of which he had doubtless seen in the Louvre. The influence of mirror-engravings became even more pro-
Ill. 98 nounced in the *plâtres gravés* of 1931–2, such as *A Nereid,* an effect which Braque achieved by darkening the surface of the plaster and then scratching his drawing into the white body beneath.

The fascination for Greek intaglios seems to have been longer-lasting, and perhaps more intense. There is a natural sympathy, to begin with, between the relief surface obtained on an intaglio and Braque's own love of *matière* plus his longing to bring every image forward to the touch. The gluey-white
Ill. 151 surface he achieved in a painted plaster like *Doves* of 1958 produces something of the effect of an intaglio image, standing out in relief against a black ground. More than this, Braque in his Cubist days had already been attracted to the round or oval format. Under the influence, one imagines, of Greek intaglios this affection for the rounded shape grew even stronger during the final decade of his life, yielding not only the small painted plasters already mentioned, but a quantity of lithographs
Ill. 158
Ills. 137–139 (*e.g., Bird in the Foliage*), and actual jewellery made to Braque's designs by the Paris jeweller Heger de Löwenfeld. (A hundred pieces of Braque's jewellery were exhibited in the Musée des Arts Decoratifs in Paris in the spring of 1963, a bare five months before the artist died.)

As a Cubist Braque was a Classical painter without trying to be. But, as the years passed, increasingly he tended to see things in more overtly Classical terms. A number of examples have already been cited of Braque's preference for Classical themes and personages. Another such case was his practice in the 1920s of supporting an arrangement of still-life objects upon monumental furniture reminiscent of Classical columns. In *Still-Life with Guitar* of 1921, for instance, the corner of a marble mantelpiece is shaped like the volute of an Ionic capital. In *The Guéridon* of 1928–9, and in many related paintings on the same theme, the central pedestal of the table is given a fluted surface in the manner of a Greek column; while in *Still-Life with Guitar and Fruit* of 1924 the tablecloth or drapery hangs down in precisely measured folds over the edge of the table in a manner even more suggestive of a fluted column.

Ill. 67
Ill. 89

Ill. 73

It would be stretching a point to claim that Braque became anything so self-conscious as a Neo-Classicist, in the sense that Derain became a Neo-Classicist. The specifically Classical elements in Braque's painting are for the most part decorative rather than structural; nostalgic – even whimsical – rather than intellectual. They stem from a natural traditionalism which asserted itself in Braque with increasing force as he grew older, and as the shock of revolution, which he had helped to cause, spread further and further from his sympathies.

Braque the revolutionary became, if not Braque the reactionary, then Braque the solitary. Braque grew deeply self-reliant, proud yet humble, orderly in his daily life, reflective, patient by nature, possessed of an intense respect for the seriousness of the painter's calling, and for the fine craftsmanship upon which a mastery of his profession depended. Braque was a man who went back to his native Normandy to live; who had himself a house built in traditional Norman country style; who designed stained-glass windows for local churches and chapels; who wore blue workmen's clothing immaculately clean and pressed; and who said proudly to Dora Vallier, 'I prepare my colours myself. I do the crushing of them.'

It is in character that this man should have made no bones about his imaginative limitations, and that he should have endeavoured to make of those limitations a source of strength. As early as 1916–17, while recovering from a severe head-wound sustained in the First World War, Braque wrote the marginal note, 'In art progress consists not in extension but in the knowledge of its limits.' (This was published along with other aphorisms in the Paris review *Nord-Sud,* December 1917.) Appropriately it was a small Chardin still-life of apples, which he saw in the Boymans–van Beuningen Museum in Rotterdam, that had impressed this truth upon him. Later he enlarged on this opinion. In a conversation held with Gaston Diehl, published in 1945, Braque explained, 'It is the limitation of means that determines style, gives rise to new forms and makes creativity possible.'

In his own *Cahier,* published in 1948, he rang yet another change: 'Restricted means engender new forms, lead to creativity, determine the style. Progress in art consists not in extending its boundaries but in knowing them better.' The identical philosophy of painting which had been conceived by him as a young Cubist still occupied Braque's mind as an old man with Cubism thirty years behind him. In this consistency of thought and brevity of expression lie what Douglas Cooper, writing in the late 1940s of Braque's contribution to painting, described as 'that calm and penetrating vision which characterizes all French art'. Braque was, more than anything else, a profoundly French painter.

CHAPTER NINE

Outward show and private meaning

Braque's still-lifes of the mid-'30s are among the gayest, the
most confident and the most colourful of all his work. *Still-
Life on a Printed Tablecloth* of 1935, *Still-Life with Mandolin, The
Purple Tablecloth, Still-Life with Fruit-dish*, all three done in
1936, and another *Still-Life with Mandolin* of 1936–8: these
paintings possess a decorative gusto absent in the solemn still-
lifes of the '20s and in the wistful products of the early '30s.
Strong reds and purples amid the familiar treacly blacks are
accompanied by a new range of pale pinks, mauves, yellows
and greens. To the old love of ornamental textures, and the old
love of ambiguity (notice the interplay between shapes that
describe actual objects, shapes that are purely decorative, shapes
that measure distances, and shapes that suggest patterns of light),
there has now been added an affection for jagged angular
forms. These first appeared in the *Bathers* series, but they play a
more satisfactory role in still-life where they balance and set
off the rounded shapes of flower-pot and fruit, mandolin and
tablecloth.

    From 1936 human figures – highly impersonal human
figures – return to inhabit these ornately decorated rooms, and
in 1938 Braque began a series of *Vanitas* still-lifes in which – as
in Dutch *memento mori* paintings of the seventeenth century – a
skull and sometimes a cross and rosary have taken the place of
the artist's customary still-life imagery. Braque himself always
denied the existence of symbolic content in his work, by
which he presumably meant that it contained no deliberate
symbolism. Yet it would be naïve to dismiss as a meaningless
coincidence the fact that, in two virtually contemporaneous
series, one features a figure or several figures engaged in either
of the two arts he loved most (painting and music), while the

Ills. 101, 102
Ills. 103

Ill. 108

99 JEAN-BAPTISTE SIMÉON CHARDIN *The White Tablecloth*

100 *The Yellow Tablecloth* 1935 ▶

Braque's preoccupation with informal still-life themes (see pages 159 *et seq*.) places him within a tradition of French painting which may be traced back through Cézanne in the nineteenth century to Chardin in the eighteenth, and even earlier. The 'Tablecloth' paintings of Braque and Cézanne trace their ancestry to such compositions as this one by Chardin, with its careless arrangement of simple things on a table. Roughly two-thirds of Braque's life's work consists of still-lifes.

second series deals with the traditional imagery of death. Was it the threat of another war (the previous one had almost killed him) that imbued Braque's painting at this moment with a sense of the polarity of beauty and destruction, and moved him to paint what he loved most and what he feared most?

134

What is clear from these two series of the late '30s is that Braque's work was growing cryptically personal. It was also becoming less literal in its presentation of material things. Braque's world had always been one of objects, in particular objects close enough to touch. Henceforth, a metaphysical note was to sound increasingly loud in Braque's painting, and for the first time images appear which either have no material existence, or else they have become detached sufficiently from that material role to introduce ideas that dwell outside the physical boundaries of Braque's theme. Just as the development of Braque's pictorial language had hitherto been in the cause of expressing matters of space and volume, these fresh images also serve the purpose of adding to our experience of space and of

101 *Still-Life on a Printed Tablecloth* 1935

102 *Still-Life with Mandolin* 1936 ▶

103 *Still-Life with Fruit-dish* 1936 ▶

Braque's still-lifes of the mid-1930s are full of sharp, jagged shapes, some of them descriptive of actual objects, more often merely ornamental.

volume – although in a different sense. The introduction during the late '30s of this metaphysical element into Braque's material world ranks as the second momentous innovation of his career (the first of course being his contribution to Cubism) and it paves the way for that series of noble and mysterious still-lifes, in some respects the summit of Braque's achievements, the *Studio* series.

136

104 *Woman with an Easel* 1936

The first, scarcely perceptible, hint of this innovation is contained in several of the series of figure compositions (already mentioned) which Braque painted between 1936 and 1939. In this important series – and it was a theme he returned to again in the '40s – dark motionless figures, single or in pairs, inhabit a richly ornamented room in which objects (a piano, an easel, chairs, a vase) are now spaced out as if to emphasize the total volume of the room instead of being grouped in the centre foreground as before. In *The Duet* of 1937 the right-hand figure

Ill. 105

105 *The Duet* 1937

plays the piano while the figure on the left holds a score. In
Woman with a Mandolin, also 1937, there is just one single
figure seated in front of a music-stand; while *The Painter and
his Model* of 1939 introduces another pair of figures. All three
contain a picture – on the wall or on the easel. Each picture is
like a coloured window opening out beyond the enclosed cell
of the room. There is strong light in the room, dividing the
figures severely into black and white, but one cannot see where
it comes from. Everywhere there is an air of tense concentration:

Ill. 109

106 *Blue Boats* 1937

107 *The Cliffs* 1938

something unseen matters, as if we should be listening to the notes of the piano, to the strings of the mandolin, or watching the progress of the picture on the easel.

The figures are impersonal, yet each composition is invaded by a human presence; invaded furthermore by shapes and colours from the inner painting on the wall which, in *The Duet* and *Woman with a Mandolin,* have overflowed the boundaries of the picture-frame and have begun to spill out into the room itself. It is as if they had no material substance but were merely lights played on to the wall by some unseen projector. These are compositions that can no longer be 'read' or explained, in the way that Braque's earlier work could be 'read'. Braque is beginning to convey a freer, more subjective, more irrational

108 *Vanitas I* 1938

experience of space than in his Cubist and immediately post-Cubist years.

Ill. 130 This metaphysical approach is echoed in an interesting precursor of the great *Studio* series of a decade later. In this painting an experience of space is conveyed in three ways. It is conveyed by the vertical division of all the objects in the room into passages of light and shadow. It is conveyed by the image of the window filled with blue and white; and it is conveyed by the purple star-like image in the picture resting on the easel which, as in the earliest compositions with figures, is freeing itself from its frame and floating into the room itself. This painting is the first hint of the perplexing bird-image that is to fly across the later *Studio* interiors and finally in the last paintings and lithographs, across the open sky.

109 *The Painter and his Model* 1939 ▶

110 *Still-Life with Garden Chair* 1939 ▶

G Braque

CHAPTER TEN

War and after

When the German armies swept through the Low Countries into France in 1940 Braque was at his summer home in Varengeville, near Dieppe. With his wife he moved south to the Limousin district and then on to the Pyrenees, where he had passed one of the key summers of Cubism with Picasso before the First World War. But once it became clear by the autumn of 1940 that the occupation of northern France had come to stay Braque, like Picasso, preferred to return to Paris: and there he remained until after the Liberation in 1944, not daring to move away again for fear the Germans might commandeer his house.

Ill. 115

Braque worked in a variety of styles and moods during the following three and a half years. He continued the *Vanitas* series, sometimes varying the sombre theme of skull, cross and rosary by the addition of a plain jug given so thick a crust of paint that it stands out in low relief (*Jug and Skull* of 1943 is one of the last of the series). Here is the apotheosis of Braque's fondness for tactile images.

Ills. 111, 116

More strongly redolent of the mood of war, and of conditions in Occupied Paris, is a group of stark interiors and still-lifes painted with a gloomy realism. Each canvas is stripped bare of decoration and ornament. There are stoves, pails, scrubbing-brushes, tables frugally laid with a single exceedingly dead fish on a plate, or a hunk of cheese, a knife and a solitary pitcher. (*e.g., In Front of the Window* and *The Kitchen Table*). Everything is depicted with a cold and unequivocal severity of line and colour, as if lyricism – imagination even – deserved no place in this climate of discomfort, and there were no songs to sing.

Braque also returned to a theme that had occupied him on and off since the years of Analytical Cubism: the pedestal-table piled high with still-life objects. Braque added several more such canvases to the already long list of *Guéridon* paintings, of which the tall upright *Still-Life on a Table* – Braque actually began this in 1939 and continued to add touches as late as 1952 – is the most colourful and the most celebrated. These paintings lack the desolate atmosphere of the realist still-lifes which are exact contemporaries. The war-time *Guéridon* pictures belong stylistically to the late 1930s. It is as though in them he were allowing the spirit of his pre-war paintings to take charge.

Ill. 143

The same is true of the poignant and remarkably beautiful figure composition of 1942 entitled *Patience*. In theme and in treatment *Patience* belongs to the group of vertically-divided interiors with figures which Braque painted between 1936 and 1939. More closely related to the realist war-time paintings is a group of small still-lifes that includes one of the artist's most popular canvases, his *Black Fish* now in the Musée National d'Art Moderne in Paris; also a larger composition that is possibly his finest achievement of this period, *Interior: The Grey Table* of 1942. This austere but serene work, also known as *Interior with Palette,* was among a group of pictures which Braque exhibited at the 1943 Salon d'Automne.

Ill. 112

Ill. 113

Ill. 114

Like several of the pre-war compositions, including *The Studio* of 1939, *Interior: The Grey Table* sounds an echo of the major *Studio* series to come. Here in simplified form lies the essence of the late Braque interior. The theme of *The Grey Table* is an intimate room, filled with human presence although no one is actually there. There is a chair pulled back as if someone had just left it; there is a table upon which rest a potted plant, a cup, fruit and the artist's own palette and brushes (again the suggestion is that they have only just been laid there); and, enlarged before the spectator's eye – so close that they have become transparent as occurs when slender objects are brought to within the minimum focal length for human sight – the curved tops of the artist's easel.

Ill. 130

Until the late '30s Braque's interiors had invariably contained a cluster of images centrally placed. Any sense of the room's volume had been created by taking 'measurements' from this

145

III *In Front of*
the Window 1942

hub of images. Now Braque has abandoned this hub and dispersed his still–life objects freely across the canvas. He suggests
the volume of a room by a different approach, by means of a
series of flat planes arranged without perspective. The position
of these planes on the canvas, and the weight of colour given
to each, now determines the distance of objects from the eye as
well as their distance from one another.

The image of the easel-top is here a very simple device for
conveying such an effect. (Braque's methods were to grow more

146

112 *Patience* 1942

involved in the *Studio* series.) The curving forms rising up
before the eye find an echo in the divisions of light and shadow
on the far wall, and so establish a relationship between the
closest and most distant parts of the picture. But being transparent they also take in all the objects which lie in between,
cutting across them, sometimes allowing them to show cleanly
through, sometimes deflecting more light on them and in
doing so reducing their substance and colour. It is an ingenious
puzzle which doubtless appealed to Braque's lifelong affection

147

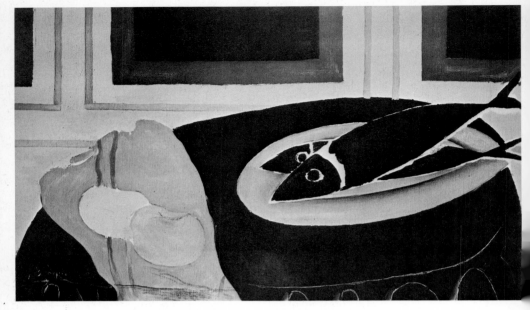

113 *The Black Fish* 1942

for the incongruous and the inexplicable. More than that, in
confusing the eye and compelling the spectator to ponder over
the complicated relationship of colour and form contained in
the picture, the puzzle intensifies the spectator's experience
of the space contained in the painting, and adds to the lyrical
subtlety of the composition. By comparison, almost identical
interiors which Braque painted without the device of the
transparent easel are relatively obvious and uninteresting.

Immediately following the liberation of Paris and Normandy
in 1944, Braque returned to Varengeville for the last autumn
of the war. In this year he began a series of interiors which
centre on what was for Braque an entirely new image, the
Ill. 118 billiard-table. The first of these incorporates the same transparent image of the easel-top, brought close up to the spectator's eye in the same manner as he used it in *Interior: The Grey
Table* painted two years earlier. Again it serves to distort and
confuse the colours and images seen through it, although less

148

radically than in the earlier painting. The billiard-table, with its broad flat surface and heavy rounded legs, performs a role in these pictures similar to that of the pedestal-table in the various *Guéridon* pictures, and this link is particularly noticeable in the upright version which Braque continued to work on until 1952, where the table is viewed end-on.

Ill. 119

But the chief appeal of the billiard-table image to Braque seems to have resided in its rectangular shape, which he was able to use to reiterate the rectangular shape of the room itself and to suggest, by means of this analogy, areas of the room not actually visible in the paintings themselves. It is a typical Braque

114 *Interior: The Grey Table* 1942
One of the greatest and most complex of Braque's war-time paintings.

115 *Jug and Skull* 1943

Braque loved mixing other materials with
oil-paint in order to achieve rich and
different textures. As here, these textures
are not always related to the images they
describe, but possess a sensuous and tactile
function of their own. This is particularly
evident in some of the late landscapes.

116 *The Kitchen Table* 1942–4

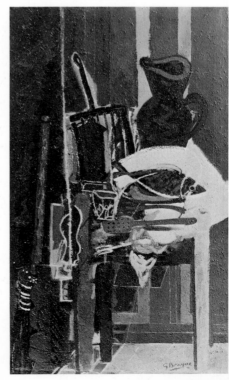

subtlety. In the 1944 version the vertical line denoting a corner *Ill. 118* of the room is made to continue down across the billiard-table and to establish a 'fold' in that table, so creating the impression that the eye is looking at it from several viewpoints within the room.

A similar 'fold' appears in the later paintings of the series. This vertical division of a flat surface to suggest a change of angle of view was a stylistic feature also of the highly orna- mented interiors of the mid-'30s such as *The Yellow Tablecloth*; *Ill. 100* but now, in the *Billiard-Table* series, by avoiding all implications of perspective, Braque has arrived at an altogether more satisfactory solution to the problem of how to create a sense of the total volume of a room. He could even achieve this sense of enclosed space with a single, fixed viewpoint; witness another masterpiece dating from that first return visit to Normandy, *The Salon,* a picture closely related to the *Billiard-Table* series *Ill. 117* in its formal arrangement of objects and in its treatment of space. On the wall there is even a picture-frame shaped curiously like Braque's billiard-tables (especially the one in *Ill.119*): and as with the star-like bird that detaches itself from the canvas in *Ill. 130* one is reminded by *The Salon* how frequently a par- ticular shape exerted a fascination on Braque some time *before* it acquired a specific meaning or a specific image. *The Salon* also reveals Braque's imaginative use of a window. It appears to be partly closed: an area of it catches the light from within the room – very much as the transparent easel-top does in *Ills. 114* and *118* – while through the open part of the window shines the dull blue of the sky.

Another field which Braque began to explore during the later days of the Second World War – it was one that was to prove richly fruitful during the last decades of his life – was colour lithography. Apart from the sixteen etchings com- missioned for Vollard's edition of Hesiod's *Theogony,* Braque had completed only six prints during the '30s, a mere five during the '20s, and about a dozen during his Cubist years. Now he formed a close association with the master-printer Fernand

117 *The Salon*
1944

118 *Billiard-Table I* 1944

119 *The Billiard-Table* 1944–52

Mourlot, and Braque's acquaintance with Mourlot's magnificently equipped workshop in Paris revealed to the painter the immense opportunities that awaited him in this field. With his natural love of the tactile, and with his respect for craftsmanship, the medium of colour-printing thereafter took on an importance for Braque only second to that of oil-paint, and it yielded some of the most lyrical products of his later years (*e.g., Ills. 142* and *146*).

Among the first colour lithographs Braque made were several done for the limited first edition of Jean Paulhan's *Braque le Patron*, printed in Paris during the German Occupation. Mourlot has described how Braque would regularly cycle across the city from his home near the Parc Montsouris in order to supervise the printing. When in 1947 Braque put his affairs in the hands of a new dealer, Aimé Maeght, he found a man who had himself been trained as a lithographer and designer-printer, and who was to stimulate and edit a continuous output of graphic work from Braque right up to 1963, the last year of his life. It was Maeght, too, who in the '50s published eight out of the ten Cubist etchings by Braque that had never been published at the time, and who in 1955 finally issued the *Hésiode-Théogonie* which had remained unpublished at Vollard's death in 1939.

Braque also took up sculpture during the war. It was at Varengeville in the last summer of peace-time that Braque had taken to picking up stones, pieces of chalk-cliff and other materials from the beach, and making little carvings of them, later to be cast in bronze. In 1920, at the time of his close association with the sculptor Henri Laurens, Braque had carved a single small figurine in plaster; while during his Analytical Cubist days with Picasso both painters had tried their hand at three-dimensional compositions in paper. But these were tentative experiments, and until the late 1930s Braque had resisted the temptation to extend his love of the tactile into the territory of sculpture, which he felt instinctively was not his. The closest that any of his serious work had come to sculpture

154

had been the decorative *plâtres gravés* of the early '30s. These were strictly reliefs, and much of the sculpture he eventually came to produce during the Second World War retains this essentially two-dimensional quality established in the *plâtres gravés*. It is sculpture intended to be seen in profile. It retains, too, much of the feeling for Archaic Greek and primitive art which had been an important source of inspiration for the *plâtres gravés*.

A certain naïve innocence affects all Braque's sculpture. Fish, bird, vase, pony, plough: here is a simple *répertoire* of playthings endowed with all the appeal a child finds in a favourite toy. They show Braque at his most gentle and appealing; at his least ambitious and least intellectual. 'If I make sculpture from time to time', he said, 'it is because it makes me break the habit of painting.' In sculpture Braque discovered a kind of nursery.

A serious illness in 1945, and another in 1947, left Braque with little time or energy to accomplish much during the three years following the end of the Second World War, except a steady output of graphic work in collaboration with Mourlot. In between the two illnesses Braque held an exhibition of recent work at the Tate Gallery in London, which he shared with Georges Rouault. And during a lengthy convalescence in 1947 he devoted a great many hours – just as he had done during his recovery from a head-wound in the First World War – to meditating on his art, and to pruning his thoughts and opinions, formed over the previous thirty years, into the form of statements and maxims illustrated with drawings. These *dicta,* profoundly valuable to an understanding of his art (I quote many of them elsewhere in this book), were published in Paris as the *Cahier de Georges Braque* in 1948 (a supplement covering the period 1947–55 appeared in 1956). In the same year Braque was selected to represent France at the Venice Biennale and won the first prize. This was the same notable Biennale at which Henry Moore was awarded the main sculpture prize and became an international celebrity overnight.

120 *The Little Horse* 1939

121 *The Pony* 1939

122 *Horse's Head* 1941–2

Braque's sculpture is never realized
quite three-dimensionally. There
is generally one 'face', or two, from
which it is intended to be seen. They
are more in the nature of free-
standing reliefs. Their textures, especially in *Ill. 122*, relate to the thick
impasto surfaces of some of the late
landscapes.

123 *Boats on the Beach* 1949

DIGRESSION 3: BRAQUE AND STILL-LIFE

Roughly two-thirds of Braque's entire output – sixty years of it – consists of still-lifes. This must be a higher proportion than is to be found in the *œuvre* of any other major painter of the twentieth century except possibly Giorgio Morandi and the short-lived Juan Gris. In fact it is doubtful if any artist since the seventeenth century painted more still-lifes than did Braque; and only Chardin and Cézanne can have extracted as much meaning and gained as much satisfaction from so limited a theme.

In this Braque is something of a paradox. As a young man in Normandy he acquired a profound love of open spaces, for countryside and sea. One of the strongest memories he retained of his youth was of long bicycle-journeys between Paris and his parents' home in Le Havre. In his old age he recalled these journeys in a group of paintings of which *The Shower* is one. *Ill. 144* Scenes of harbours and estuaries are among the earliest surviving paintings from his hand. This love of landscape, of water and broad skies, seems if anything to have deepened during the latter half of his life. Many of the most lyrical compositions of his last thirty-three years are endowed with a spirit of undisguised enthusiasm for the open air. A number are illustrated in this book: among them *Boats on the Beach, Dieppe* of 1929, *Ill. 94* *The Cliffs* of 1938, *Boats on the Beach* of 1949, *The Black Boat* *Ills. 107, 123* of 1958, and Braque's last completed picture *The Weeding* *Ill. 154* *Machine* of 1961–3. *Ill. 160*

All his life, what is more, the question of how to represent the idea or sensation of space in only two dimensions was foremost in Braque's mind. Why then, for a man of such preoccupations, should still-life become the theme with which he most closely identified himself?

This is less of a paradox than it first appears to be. The simplest answer may lie in the phrase of Braque quoted before: 'Compelled by the desire to go further towards an expression of space, I wanted to avail myself of the faculty of touch.' These sentiments are echoed in a statement from the artist's own

Cahier: 'It is not enough to make what one paints visible. One must do more, make it tangible.' Braque's preoccupation with space was in effect of two kinds: it was a lyrical response to open space – harbours, beaches, fields, skies – which the eye could enjoy and the spirit delight in; and it was a more profound, more intellectual concern to represent space that lay in a closely defined area, separating yet uniting objects that lie within the reach of a man's hand. Still-life was Braque's microcosm: it was the world at his fingertips.

There exists, then, an unusual interplay in Braque's work – I am tempted to call it a tussle – between what is wide open and what is enclosed, between what is free and what is restrained and, by extension, between what is profoundly emotional – which a great deal of Braque's work is – and yet pretends not to be.

'I love the rule which corrects the emotion', Braque wrote in a series of 'Pensées et Reflexions' (published in Pierre Reverdy's review *Nord-Sud*, Paris, December 1917): 'Nobility grows from contained emotion.'

Ill. 24 The lifelong series of still-lifes began in 1908, in the first full year of Cubism. *Still-Life with Fruit-dish and Plate* is among the earliest of these compositions. It is very Cézanne-influenced, and very close to contemporary still-lifes by Picasso whom Braque had encountered in Paris the previous autumn. Within a further eighteen months the still-life theme had become the hub of Analytical Cubism. Much as Cézanne – so it is said – found it convenient to test his pictorial ideas by treating objects that were close to hand, both Braque and Picasso (at this time) made their revolutionary experiments in conceptual art with the simplest and more familiar objects in their immediate environment.

In doing so they introduced to still-life painting an entirely fresh *répertoire* of day-to-day objects, and in the process succeeded in revitalizing an art which, for all the boldness of Cézanne and the rough handling administered by Van Gogh (he had deemed a pair of old boots to be a fit subject for a still-life) still remained within the politely contrived conventions tailored to French manners before the Revolution.

Some of the objects that begin to appear in the still-lifes of Picasso and Braque from 1909 onwards seem to hark back quite deliberately to the eighteenth century, in particular the various musical instruments (violins, mandolins, lutes, clarinets, pianos, harps, as well as sheets of printed music in which Braque's work abounds). Other images introduce a more contemporary and informal note: bottles of wine, vodka and rum, kitchen-knives, dice, pipe, playing cards, newspapers, tickets, cinema-posters, beer-labels. With these objects as the instruments of the Cubist experiment, still-life in the twentieth century developed so far from genteel formality as to yield some of the most intimate and intense painting in modern times. Cézanne, followed by Braque and Picasso, helped to raise it from a minor to a major art.

Braque remained above all else a painter of still-life, whereas Picasso of course did not. There is not even much change in Braque's subject-matter after the Cubist years (apart from more frequent images of fruit): it is the manner of presentation that alters. The same mandolin, the same musical score, the same goblet, pipe and bottle recur – alongside new images such as fruit, the artist's own palette and brushes, a skull and cross, a vase of flowers occasionally, a plate of fish, a lamp, an easel. The *répertoire* extends a little: some images drop out and fresh ones replace them: but by and large the scene was to remain the same until the artist's death at the age of eighty-one.

To Braque, as Douglas Cooper has observed, reality meant the reality of *things*; whereas to Picasso reality has always resided in experience (most frequently an experience of *people*). With Braque experience impinged upon the imagination only through something that seemed to him fundamental, which was a grasp of the physical existence of objects. He liked the permanence and impassivity of material things.

'*L'objet, c'est tout*,' he would maintain. And in his *Cahier* he elaborated on this: 'The painter thinks in shapes and colours.

The object is the poetic element.' The principal difference between Braque's and Picasso's treatment of objects is clear from the different manner in which they each undertook large cluttered paintings on the theme of their own studios. Picasso's *Studio* pictures, executed at the Villa La Californie in Cannes during the mid-1950s, are numerous and display every sign of having been completed rapidly, often in a single day. The Art Nouveau French windows with palm trees beyond, potted rubber plants, easels, canvases, chairs, cupboards and other furniture which crowd each painting are treated decoratively, with a strong fascination for the oddities and contrasts in form which they offer. Objects are never endowed with a private significance or spiritual meaning. What does emerge is a strong total experience of the room itself as a kind of magic workshop, flooded with the artist's own presence just as it is with light.

Braque's *Studio* series, on the other hand, done between 1949 and 1956, is relatively small in number – there are eight large canvases in all – and each painting records a long process of thought and meditation. Single paintings occupied him several years. There is nothing decorative about them; neither is there any attempt to express the living atmosphere of the studio, or any experience of the moment. Braque's studio is shown as a place of dark recesses, where dream and observation merge, a place crowded with plain objects that have grown so familiar that they have begun to shed their identity and have become associated – confused – with other things, a place where a man may lose himself in thought among those possessions with which his imagination is most closely identified. Picasso's studio is a scene of action, a well-lit stage dominated by the presence of the painter himself. Braque's studio is a retreat for the purposes of contemplation, and a sanctuary for precious objects with which the artist's life is most naturally associated.

Braque's love of objects was partly a straightforward affection for everyday things. But the everyday things he chose possess two qualities in common. They have a strongly tactile appeal, and they carry associations with pleasures that are also strongly tactile: eating, drinking, playing (whether cards or music), cooking, smoking and so on. It is interesting that Braque, like Cézanne, rarely painted flowers (although when he did so the result could be triumphant), perhaps because flowers do not offer any such appeal to the touch. What Braque loved were objects which could be brought to life by the process of touch, whose living function depends on the human hand – cups, cards, dice, fruit, the artist's own palette and, of course, musical instruments.

Braque's love of music was second only to his love of painting, and this is reflected in the long series of compositions with musical instruments which he completed between *Guitar and Fruit-dish* of 1909 and *The Duet* of 1937, after which they *Ills. 33, 105* all but vanish from his work. 'Music' was one of those words ('poetry' was another) which Braque, like Kandinsky, was inclined to apply to painting in a loose sense when searching for a non-literary explanation of the importance to him of a particular form, or the essential relationship that he felt lay between two areas of a canvas. Thus, 'A vase gives a shape to the void, and music to silence', he wrote cryptically in his *Cahier*: or again, to Dora Vallier, '. . . you put a blob of yellow here, and another at the further edge of the canvas: straight away a *rapport* is established between them. Colour acts in the way that music does, if you like.' 'There is more sensitivity in technique than in the rest of the picture', he went on.

Any artist in seventeenth-century Holland, in what was the Golden Age of still-life painting, would certainly have agreed with Braque that technique came first, but they would not have been talking about the same thing at all. Where seventeenth-century specialists in still-life – Claesz, Heda, de Heem, van Beyeren, van der Aelst, Rachel Ruysch and many others – strove to perfect techniques which heightened the lifelikeness of their compositions (*trompe l'œil* was the ultimate achievement in this direction), by technique Braque meant something that was free from the cult of naturalism, and altogether more sensuous. Braque's interest was *matière* – actual substance – not

163

surface polish. Love of dramatic realism, which Northern painters had taken over from Caravaggio, had no place in Braque's intentions whatever.

It is true that a small group of *Vanitas* paintings which Braque undertook in the late '30s and early '40s may point to a certain interest in Netherlandish art. He would certainly have been familiar with the earliest-known painting on such a theme, a fifteenth-century work by Rogier van der Weyden hanging in the Louvre. A Dutch seventeenth-century still-life artist who specialized in *Vanitas* compositions, Hendrick van Steen-wijk, may conceivably have interested Braque as well, and one or two tenuous similarities can be made out between the work of the two painters. What is more probable is that the inspiration for Braque's *memento mori* compositions, if historical at all, lay in the moralistic still-lifes which Jansenist philosophy caused to be something of a cult in seventeenth-century France. More likely still is that they go no further back than the mounting threat of the Second World War, aided by the recollection that Cézanne had himself tried his hand at a *Vanitas* painting in 1904.

Cézanne was probably the artist most singly responsible for Braque's love of still-life. With Cézanne a new density, a new sense of structure and rhythm, a new toughness, came into still-life. But if Cézanne was Braque's immediate mentor in the art of still-life, for the master to whom he came closest in spirit one must retrace a further century and a half, glancing respect-fully on the way at earlier nineteenth-century practitioners of still-life such as Manet, Corot and Courbet, and at interesting provincial figures like Ribot, Vollon, Bonvin and Monticelli - to Chardin.

The most distinguished independent figure in French eighteenth-century art, Chardin was not the first to endow still-life with the warmth of human feelings: something of his intimacy and informality was anticipated by earlier French artists of still-life, notably Baugin a century before. Chardin was none the less the first to raise still-life above the level of a decorative art, and this he achieved by perceiving that inanimate objects with strong human associations could be grouped no less harmoniously than human beings could be grouped. Dutch seventeenth-century still-life painters *contrived* their compositions. So did Desportes and Oudry in France. Chardin possessed the much rarer gift for sensing where objects belonged most naturally, as if they had taken up those positions of their own choice. He achieved, in short, that sense of instinctive rightness which, at their best, Cézanne and Braque achieved too, and which Braque referred to as the 'poetic' element in art.

Add to those formal harmonies which Chardin achieved the equally marvellous harmonies he obtained with colour, and one arrives at the two territories in which the still-lifes of Cézanne and Braque are closer to those of Chardin than to the work of any other painter. Chardin, like Braque, was a man who imposed limitations on his scope and made a virtue of them. Cézanne's tribute to Chardin lies in those still-lifes of the early 1870s (the La Caze Collection, including twelve Chardins, had been acquired by the Louvre in 1869) with objects piled upon white tablecloths that are ruffled into shadows to allow an infinite subtlety of whites and greys. Braque's life-work is his tribute to Chardin; and if one seeks to pin-point the debt, then the long series of *Tablecloth* paintings which he undertook in the '30s and '40s, seem to have the most of Chardin in them.

Chardin's own *White Tablecloth,* now in the collection of the Art Institute of Chicago, may be said to be Braque's earliest and most distinguished ancestor.   *Ill. 99*

CHAPTER ELEVEN

The Studio paintings

During the course of 1948 Braque, now fully recovered from his serious illness, embarked upon what was to prove a culminating achievement of his post-Cubist years: the *Studio* series which was to occupy his energies more or less continuously until 1956. This series consisted finally of eight paintings, all of them large except the first, and all of them dealing with the twin themes that had increasingly engaged his imagination since the *Guéridon* paintings of the late '20s: the enclosed space of a room, and the objects in it which enable that space to be measured and experienced.

Braque had already taken his own studio as an explicit subject in 1939, and the first of this new series (completed in 1949) was a quiet beginning, no more ambitious than its pre-
Ill. 124 decessor. *Studio I* is, if anything, simpler and less interesting than the figure compositions of the late '30s, than the *Billiard-Table* paintings, or than the other war-time interiors such as
Ill. 114 *The Grey Table,* all of which contributed to a build-up of ideas that were to result in the post-war *Studio* series.

Studio I, like several of the '30s figure compositions, contains a painting within a painting – actually more than one – and what seems to have concerned Braque most has been to offset the black silhouette of a jug in one of these 'inner' paintings with a similar jug shown as a flat silhouette in white in another 'inner' painting above and behind it. The effect is to achieve a straightforward play of two flat rectangles, one with a suggestion of volume and one without, displayed in a highly restricted space. By its simplicity of form and purpose *Studio I* does not truly belong to the remainder of the series, and in it Braque has explored none of the intricate labyrinths of space which distinguished the remaining seven.

166

124 *Studio I* 1949

Of these seven, six form a distinct cycle: Nos. *II, III, IV, VI, VIII* and *IX*. *Studio V* Braque considered to lie apart from the others. *Studio VII* no longer exists, having been re-worked to become *Studio IX*. It was in this cycle of six paintings that Braque made his last major statement concerning the experience of an enclosed space realized in terms of a two-dimensional surface. It is demonstrative of the deep personal significance contained in these paintings that he should have chosen, as the setting in which to explore this theme, the place

Ills. 125, 126, 127, 135, 136, 147

167

125 *Studio II* 1949

126 *Studio III* 1949 ▶

127 *Studio IV* 1949 ▶

where he had worked in private for twenty years (both his studios in Paris and Varengeville were arranged the same way), the room that through those years had fed his thoughts, held his secrets, had drawn its character – its very shape even – from the palettes, brushes, tubes of colour, easels and the scattered canvases waiting to pronounce themselves one day finished: the room that was the very world of his art. Picasso, for his most intimate statements, has invariably painted the face of the women he loved. Braque chose his own workshop.

168

◄ 128 *The Purple Tablecloth* 1936

◄ 129 *Still-Life with Flowers and Fruit* 1938–9

130 *The Studio* 1939

131 *Still-Life: Mandolin II* 1939–40

The art historian John Richardson frequented this workshop during the years when Braque was engaged on the *Studio* series, and this is how he described the place, in the June 1955 *Burlington Magazine*: 'Carefully disposed on easels and stands, against the neutral background of a curtain which divides the room in half, is ranged a display of Braque's current painting, framed and unframed, in various stages of completion: likewise drawings and lithographs are methodically laid out on the floor. Elsewhere canvases and frames are stacked, a sketch-book lies open on a lectern, small tables are neatly piled with supplies of artist's materials, while others are covered with pots, vases, musical instruments, pieces of sculpture, *objets trouvés*, plants, flowers, and the like, which the painter uses without actually copying in his still-lifes. The total effect is that of an elaborately arranged composition waiting to be incorporated into a picture.'

In the *Studio* series Braque achieved an ultimate reconciliation of the material and the immaterial; a reconciliation between tangible objects that mark out the actual space in a room, and images and shapes with no material existence which are used to provoke thoughts and sensations concerning space generally. They are at once an elaborate record of observed reality and an interpretation of feelings which long acquaintance with that reality has implanted deep.

Already in several of the interiors of the '30s and early '40s a metaphysical element had entered Braque's paintings – colours and shapes detaching themselves from a picture on the wall, the image of the four-pointed star seeming to transform itself into that of a bird, the strange transparent image of Braque's own easel that exercised such mysterious power over those forms within its outline. Now, in the *Studio* paintings, this metaphysical element has become dominant. These pictures can no longer be described as realistic accounts of a place or of objects. Images have no naturalistic role, but belong to the realm of ideas.

Ills. 125–127   In *Studio II, III* and *IV*, for instance, the insubstantial image of a large bird in flight, evoking a sense both of open space and

172

132 *The Night* 1951

In the '50s and '60s Braque sometimes returned to the careful stipple technique he had used as a Fauvist fifty years before and during the height of Analytical Cubism.

of free movement, is woven between the forest of vertical planes by means of which the interior space of Braque's own studio is described. The bird threads its way through the architecture of each picture like a dream that has lingered on into the fabric of the day; whereas in *Studio VIII* and *Studio IX* the bird is clearly a painted bird belonging to a canvas in Braque's studio. (There was in fact just such a painting there, now destroyed, at the time Braque was beginning the *Studio* series.) 'Take the birds which you'll have noticed in so many of my recent paintings', Braque said to John Richardson in a

Ills. 147, 136

173

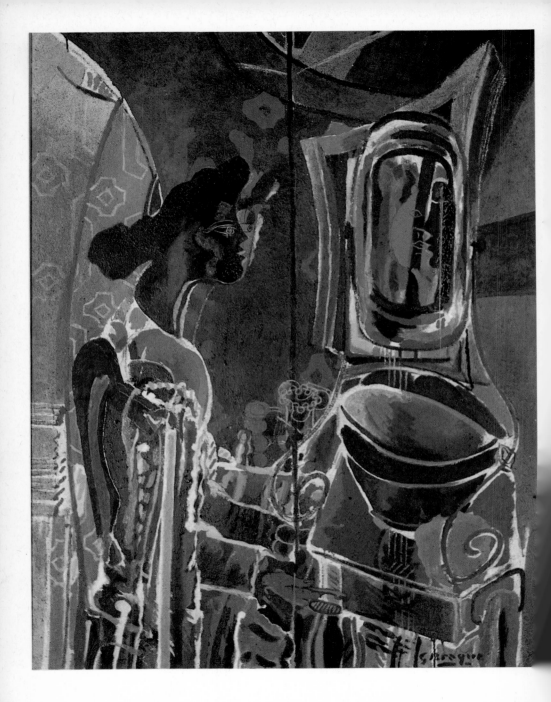

◀ 133 *Woman at the Mirror* 1945

134 *Helios V, blue-violet* 1948

statement published in *The Observer* of 1 December 1957; 'I never thought them up, they just materialized of their own accord, they were born on the canvas; that is why it is absurd to read any sort of symbolic significance into them.'

It was never intended, then, to be a real bird. With that love of puzzle and incongruity, conspicuous in his work since the *trompe l'œil* nail appeared in *Violin and Palette* and *Violin and Pitcher* of 1910, Braque is deliberately playing a *game* of reality, combining the recognizable contents of his studio (pots, jugs, palettes, tables, easels, etc.) with images which are 'born on the canvas': the bird, the arrow in *Studio II,* and the green and orange doily in *Studio IV.* Braque was able to achieve this blend of material image with immaterial because the distinction between them was no longer one he recognized. He had long since ceased to paint directly from life: the only reality that counted for him was the reality of something fully experienced and remembered.

'I have made a great discovery', he told Richardson; ' – I no longer believe in anything. Objects do not exist for me except in so far as a harmonious relationship exists between them and myself.' Images, like the space they inhabit, tend now to be fluid in Braque's work because that 'harmonious relationship' is one that seeks correspondences between one form and another, and the metamorphosis of one form into another. The relationship, in the *Studio* series, between the (concrete) image of the palette and that of the (unreal) bird demonstrates this principle of metamorphosis very clearly. One is a concrete image, the other a creation of the painter's imagination; yet the form of one at times blends into the form of the other. In *Studio II, III, IV, VIII* and *IX* these two images occupy virtually the same positions in relation to one another, the bird above and the palette below or a little to the left. In *Studio II* and *III* there is no obvious connection between the two. But in *Studio IV* the bird in flight has assumed a rounded shape very like that of the palette in *Studio III,* as if the bird itself has become the artist's palette taken wing. In

Ills. 35, 36

Ill. 125
Ill. 127

Ills. 125, 126
Ill. 127

Studio VI both palette and bird have grown amorphous, but   *Ill. 135*
now Braque has introduced a second bird, an incongruously
alert and lifelike hen perched upon the artist's easel just in front
of the amorphous figure of the bird in flight.

All this is most puzzling. This second bird may be yet
another case of deliberate incongruity. In all probability there
was no conscious reasoning behind it, nor behind the metamorphoses that take place between bird-image and palette-
image. It is consistent with Braque's method of working that
they should simply have developed that way as each painting
developed. If one seeks for a further explanation it must lie
in Braque's concern at this time to dissolve the distinction
between the material and the immaterial image (see his statement to Richardson), and to retreat more than ever from the
position of copying life and obeying its natural laws.

As I have suggested, it can scarcely have been chance that
led Braque to select, for his final statement about enclosed space,
the theme of his own studio. Here in his own workshop he was
at liberty to represent images as being of his own plastic inven-
tion; images that hint at reality, comment on reality, but never
actually copy or belong to reality. Hence, most likely, the bird
that at one stage takes its form from the space of the artist's own
palette. Moreover, this bird is very much Braque's personal
emblem: a creature that moves freely through space (and the
experience of space was Braque's first and last concern as a
painter); also a creature born on the canvas, made of colours
carried on a palette. And though this bird may seem to liberate
itself from the canvas, as it has done in *Studio VIII*, it remains   *Ill. 147*
the artist's personal creation, and he is free to re-design and
reinterpret its form according to the needs of his picture, which
is precisely what Braque has done in *Studio IX* by painting over   *Ill. 136*
the original simple image of a bird in flight and substituting for
it a fractured pattern of a bird caught in a web of yellow and
grey shapes and lines.

Only one of the eight *Studio* pictures is brightly coloured:
Studio VIII. The others are painted in that infinitely varied and

177

135 *Studio VI* 1950–1

136 *Studio IX* 1952–6

In an earlier state this painting was known as *Studio VII*. The bird image
that runs through most of the *Studio* series has become, in the revised
version, an almost unrecognizable array of broken-up shapes in the top
right of the painting.

mellow range of sunless blacks and browns, blue-greys and silver-greys, at which Braque excelled. As in his Analytical Cubist pictures, Braque avoided colours that might have disturbed the careful play of light and shadow of which each painting is composed. In *Studio II, III, IV* and *VI*, each painted on black-primed canvas, this division of light and shade is achieved by means of a dense field of verticals that chop up the picture into a multitude of narrow avenues cutting their way across the objects cluttering the room. In *Studio VI* these slender verticals have receded in favour of more rounded images of pots, jars and lamps whose shadowy forms seem to swell into the dark spaces of the room one behind another. In *Studio VIII* of 1954–5 the vertical shafts of light and shade are even further in the background, and the central area of the picture is now occupied by a complicated interleaving of flat planes, painted in strong colours in a manner echoing the stained-glass window Braque had recently completed for a chapel at Varengeville. Similar echoes of his work in stained glass are to be found in *Studio IX* of 1952–6, with its range of sombre greys illuminated by patches of yellow, pink and golden brown.

This involved – and unresolved – painting, divided into four distinct areas each of which treats the experience of space and volume in a different way, represents at once the conclusion and the disintegration of the *Studio* theme. The thin vertical divisions into light and shade, the full-bodied shadowy forms, the image of the bird broken and re-assembled out of jagged fragments, the flat areas of strong colour: they are all here in one picture, but already the sense of the volume of an entire mysterious room has all but vanished.

DIGRESSION 4: METAPHOR AND METAMORPHOSIS

In the final phase of Cubism Braque's method of presenting the reality of objects switched from analyzing those objects to finding metaphors of them. That is to say, description gave way to hint. The descriptive areas of such paintings as *Still-Life with*

Playing Cards of 1913 and *The Musician* of 1917–18 are shadowy *Ills. 54, 60*
and secondary compared to the textured and coloured areas
which play a metaphorical or 'synthetic' role. And this change
in approach is even clearer in Braque's *papiers collés*, such as
Aria de Bach and *The Clarinet*, both 1913, *Bottle and Glass*, 1914, *Ills. 52, 28,*
and the Picasso-esque *Guitar and Clarinet* of 1918. The split *55, 61*
between colour and image is now nearly complete.

From the early 1920s onwards Braque's approach to his
subject changes again. Abandoning Cubist fragmentation and
abandoning metaphor he returned to what gives the impression
of being a conventional, literal treatment of images once again.
Yet, while it is true that Braque's images are now more naturalistic, more straightforward, his interests appear to lie elsewhere.
Braque has begun to employ the limited *répertoire* of shapes that
are to become so familiar in his later work – bottle, fruit, dish,
table and so on – but he has begun to treat them as archetypal
shapes. In this way he has managed to dissociate each shape from
a specific image just sufficiently to apply it to other and quite
different images. In other words the appeal to Braque of a
particular form, and of a particular way of painting that form,
has come to precede in importance any particular image which
that form may chance to represent.

I believe this to be among the key changes which register
Braque's emergence from Cubism. A straightforward early
example is the manner in which the anatomy of *Reclining Nude*, *Ill. 75*
painted in 1924, relates to a number of contemporary still-lifes,
among them the magnificent *Bottle, Glass and Fruit* of the same *Ill. 74*
year, and the Tate Gallery's *Still-Life* of 1925. The shapes *Ill. 82*
formed by the woman's breasts and by the muscles of her
stomach are more or less exactly those of the fruit in the other
compositions: the treatment is likewise identical. Braque's
interest at this time lay not in the nature, or substance, of fruit
or of breasts, but in the small vocabulary of archetypal shapes
to which those images conform.

Later this independence of shape from image becomes more
clearly stated. In the early 1930s Braque executed a series of

still-lifes characterized by limp curvilinear forms described by means of thin washes of colour, over which the slender outlines of the familiar cups, dishes, bottles, fruit, musical instruments and table-tops have been drawn in, rather in the manner associated with Ben Nicholson. *Large Brown Still-Life* and *The Grey Table* are among the best of this group. In both cases, the latter in particular, the large curvilinear forms reminiscent of those in the contemporary wood-reliefs of Jean Arp appear to play only the most vague descriptive role and yet to echo the shapes of mandolin and fruit-dish, table and goblet, which lie superimposed upon them.

Ill. 93
Ill. 96

Again, in the ornate 'baroque' interiors which Braque turned to later in the 1930s – *The Yellow Tablecloth, Still-Life with Mandolin* and *Still-Life with Fruit-dish* – the shapes of actual objects are echoed almost exactly in the decorative patterns which surround these objects. In *The Yellow Tablecloth* the contorted form of Braque's favourite mandolin is repeated over and over again in the design of the tablecloth beneath. In *Still-Life with Fruit-dish* the sharply-pointed ornamentation on the glass goblet is picked up by the design of the tablecloth, and a jagged and spotted leaf lying in a dish on the table has become the motif of the wallpaper behind. The same wallpaper motif recurs in *Still-Life with Mandolin,* only this time it picks up the tooth-edged shape of the fruit (or are they nuts?) in a dish on the table, as well as the jagged pattern round the mandolin.

Ill. 100
Ills. 102, 103

Probably the most striking example of metamorphosis in Braque's work – and it is one that we can actually watch developing – is the harmony which grows up in the *Studio* paintings of the late 1940s and early 1950s between the image of a bird in flight and the image of the artist's palette. On page 176 I have recounted in some detail how the two images appear to borrow from one another and grow alike. In the present context it may be relevant to point out that the four paintings in which this relationship exists are: *Studio II, Studio III, Studio IV* and *Studio VI.* To probe more deeply would be to run the danger of arriving at an answer a great deal more explicit than the painter himself intended. 'To define a thing' – the wry axiom is from Braque's *Cahier* – 'is to substitute the definition for that thing.' Thus are all writers on Braque warned to tread warily over his secrets with our words.

Braque believed in intuition and he believed in mystery. The whole process of metamorphosis in his work is closely bound up with such beliefs. He held emphatically that a work of art stripped of mystery becomes stripped of *poetry*, 'the quality I value above all else in art', he told John Richardson (*The Observer*, 1 December 1957). 'I would say that it was "poetry" which distinguishes the Cubist paintings which Picasso and I arrived at intuitively from the lifeless sort of painting which those who followed us tried, with such unfortunate results, to arrive at theoretically.'

So he preferred a picture not to be 'understood', in the sense that it could be described and explained. It was virtually Braque's definition of a good picture that it could not be. The quality of mystery which he deeply respected in a work of art was for him the fruit of meditation: it was the outcome of his practice of leaving an unfinished canvas in his studio often for years, and of allowing fresh ideas to work on him gradually, once all associations with whatever prompted its beginnings had been rinsed from the memory, and the painting had begun to assert a life of its own. Hence the (ultimately) inexplicable nature of the metamorphoses which Braque's shapes often undergo. He could not possibly account for them, only explain (in his *Cahier*) that 'it is necessary to reach a certain temperature sufficient to make things malleable'; and, in answer to questions put to him by Zervos, 'Art is polymorphic. A picture appears to each onlooker under a different guise.'

Art is inexplicable, Braque held. Therefore 'whatever is valuable in painting is precisely what one is incapable of talking about' (recorded by Gaston Diehl and published in *Les Problèmes de la Peinture*, Paris, 1945). 'Conformism begins with definition', says Braque in his *Cahier*: 'the function of art is to disturb. Science reassures.' 'There are certain mysteries, certain secrets in my own work', Braque confided to Richardson, 'which even I don't understand, nor do I try to do so.' And, 'Critics should help people see for themselves; they should never try to define things, or impose their own explanations, though I admit that if – as nearly always happens – a critic's explanations serve to increase the general obscurity that's all to the good. French poets are particularly helpful in this respect. . . . *Il faut toujours augmenter le trouble.*'

Braque may have gone to some pains to dissuade anyone from understanding his work in literary terms: none the less he offered a few more positive indications of his point of view. 'I will try to explain what I mean by metamorphosis', he said to John Richardson who visited him while the artist was engaged on his *Studio* series. 'For me no object can be tied down to any one sort of reality. A stone may be part of a wall, a piece of sculpture, a lethal weapon, a pebble on a beach or anything else you like. . . . When you ask me whether a particular form in one of my paintings depicts a woman's head, a fish, a vase, a bird, or all four at once, I can't give you a categorical answer, for this "metamorphic" confusion is fundamental to the poetry.' It is a confusion of identities not dissimilar to that which the Surrealists strove to achieve by more intellectual and radical means – the confusion between human, animal, mechanical, vegetable and crystalline forms to be found in the work of Max Ernst, similar ambiguities present in the wood-reliefs of Jean Arp, the cryptic early sculpture of Giacometti and the bone-landscapes of Tanguy. One may cite, too, in this context the hybrid forms (part-landscape and part-human figure) that make up an important corpus of Henry Moore's sculpture.

To draw these parallels is to associate Braque with un-expected company: indeed the comparisons are largely superficial, prompted by similarities in treatment of forms and images rather than by any profound point of contact. There was never anything Surrealist in Braque: his interests were altogether more earthy. He never cultivated the irrational, merely let it take its course. Even the strong metaphysical ele-

184

ment present in his later work – the Braque of the *Studio* series and of the *Bird* paintings and lithographs – springs from nothing more strange or irrational than a love of paint itself: its colours, its textures, the way a stroke added here and there can transform one image into quite another. Towards the end of his life Braque talked on this theme to Georges Charbonnier (*Le Monologue du Peintre*, Paris, 1959): 'by using a white paint applied to the canvas I make a napkin. But I am sure the white shape is something conceived before knowing what it was to become. This means that a certain transformation has taken place. . . . In a painting, what counts is the unexpected.'

Symptomatic of this fascination for materials, and for the mysterious paths into which those materials may lead an artist as he works, was Braque's solemn claim that a canvas must always be prepared with the utmost care because it is like the foundations of a house. He might equally well have said it was like the beginnings of a journey, because increasingly as he grew older Braque undertook a painting in the spirit of an expedition into the unknown, a voyage with a fixed starting-point but with no defined aim or destination. 'It is the act of painting, not the finished painting, which counts', he told Richardson, speaking as if he were Willem De Kooning or Jackson Pollock. To Dora Vallier he explained: 'I am always working on a number of canvases at one time, eight, ten. . . . I take years to finish them, but I look at them each day. . . . You see the advantage of not working from real life – the apples would be rotten long before I completed my canvas. . . . I find that it is important to work slowly. Anyone who looks at such a canvas will follow the same path the artist took, and he will experience that it is the path which counts more than the outcome of it, and that the route taken has been the most interesting part.'

In short, the artist's production of a painting, as well as the spectator's enjoyment of that painting, must be a continuous and ever-changing experience. 'With age', Braque wrote in his *Cahier*, 'art and life are one and the same thing.' Painting became, for Braque, a metaphor of the process of living.

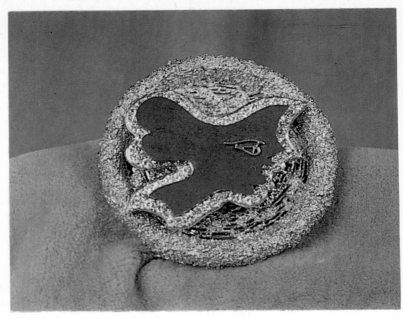

137 *Head in Profile (Hecate II)* 1962–3

138 *Hades* 1962–3

139 *Pelias and Neleus* 1962–3

When Braque became too ill to work on a large scale, he accepted the invitation to make a number of designs for jewellery. These jewels were exhibited in Paris in the spring of 1963, a few months before the artist's death.

CHAPTER TWELVE

Last works

During the period of seven years when Braque was engaged on the *Studio* series, he was also fulfilling a number of taxing commissions. In 1949 Louis Jouvet asked him to design the décor for a production of Molière's *Tartuffe*. In 1952–3 Braque completed a large ceiling decoration for the Etruscan Gallery of the Louvre, commissioned by Georges Salles who was then Director of French Museums. And in the following year he executed panels for the living-room of his dealer, Aimé Maeght, at Saint-Paul-de-Vence, as well as completing his series of stained-glass windows at Varengeville. During the winter of 1953–4 Braque also suffered his third serious illness since the end of the war.

The combination of illness, large-scale commissions, and his own painting series, left Braque with little time and few energies to undertake other large-scale work during these years. His output of small graphic work, on the other hand, continued. He executed a number of etchings during the 1950s, some on his new *Bird* theme, and some with Classical subjects; and he continued to explore the graphic medium most congenial to his lyrical talents, that of colour lithography. *Leaves, Colour, Light,* often regarded as his outstanding work in this medium, was published in 1953. And in these late lithographs, frequently containing that emblem of flight, the simplified image of a bird, Braque drew remarkably close to the strong plain statements in colour made by Matisse in the *papiers découpés* done in the late 1940s and early 1950s just before the artist's death.

Ill. 146

Braque did produce two last major figure compositions during these years: *The Night* in 1951 and *Ajax* in 1955. The first of these ranks among Braque's most forceful paintings. The

Ills. 132, 148

141 *The Cornfield* 1951

142 *Amaryllis* 1958

143 *Still-Life on a Table* 1939–52

tall alert figure of the woman with flowing hair, standing out-lined against a dark sky, has a dramatic presence, a wild – almost heroic – quality most untypical of Braque's figures, normally so impassive and remote. Then, in contrast to the dramatic treat-ment of the head, much of the figure is painted in delicate flecks of grey-blue and pale buff, recalling the tonal shading employed by Braque in the Analytical Cubist compositions of forty years earlier, such as *The Portuguese* and *Woman Reading*. *Ajax*, more overtly inspired by the legends of pre-Classical Greece, is stylistically an altogether different work. The con-tinuous wiry line by which the striding figure of the warrior is depicted relates the painting closely to Braque's *plâtres gravés* of

Ills. 42, 44

144 *The Shower* 1952

145 *Design for a Ceiling in the Louvre, II* 1953

A Matisse-like simplicity of design, imagery and colour characterizes much of Braque's late work.

the early '30s, although here the predominantly linear technique has been embellished by smears of green, blue, yellow and brown oil-paint, and a strong red (a suggestion of blood?) flicked on with the brush in a manner, again uncharacteristic of Braque, which suggests that he was momentarily intrigued by the fashion of the day, *tachisme*.

After the upsurge of creative activity during the years 1949–56, Braque's output in the last phase of his life not surprisingly slowed down. He was now seventy-four, and dogged by ill-health which latterly made the sheer physical effort of painting difficult for him. He continued to produce some of his most sumptuous colour lithographs and colour etchings after 1956 – modest in scale, direct and unadorned in design, vibrant in colour (*The Amaryllis* of 1958 is among the best of these) – *Ill. 142* as well as a steady flow of cabinet-sized flower-pieces and still-lifes. (Braque's familiar chamber music) of a Matisse-like simplicity of design and richness of paint surface.

146 *Leaves, Colour, Light*
(definitive state) 1954

Braque's interest in the newly developed medium of colour-lithography was productive of some of his most successful work in the '50s and early '60s. *Leaves, Colour, Light* is an excellent example.

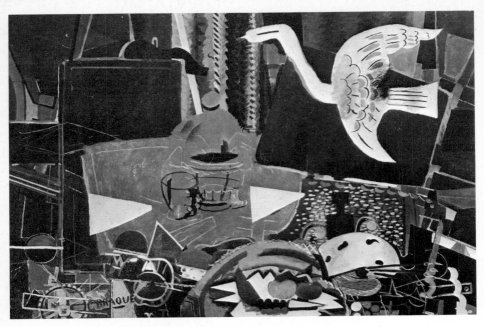

147 *Studio VIII* 1954–5

148 *Ajax* 1955

149 *Bird returning to its Nest* 1956 ▶

150 *The Nest in the Foliage* 1958 ▶

151 *Doves (black background)* 1958

The most substantial body of work he achieved during the late '50s and early '60s concerns once again Braque's long pre-occupation to present space as a tangible substance by means of pigment. Only now he has demolished the walls that formerly enclosed that space. Two earlier series of paintings have a direct bearing on the ethereal compositions of Braque's old age. They are his beach pictures (culminating in the *Ill. 123* superb *Boats on the Beach* of 1949) together with related open-air paintings of the early '50s, and of course the *Studio* series of 1949–56. From the first of these Braque derived a fresh interest and confidence in depicting *open* space (as distinct from space within a room) and in adopting what amounts to a literal approach to landscape. From the second he took that enigmatic and powerful image of the bird in flight, emblem of movement and of space itself and the embodiment of all that Braque felt to be spiritual.

In the simplest possible manner the metaphysical and the physical merge in these last paintings of birds and sky. Horizon, sky, cosmic space even, are now tactile as formerly Braque had made a jug or a lemon tactile; yet the bird that wings across these clotted skies remains an unreal and insubstantial thing, an image from a dream.

A group of etchings to illustrate the book *Cinq Sapates* by his friend the poet Francis Ponge in 1950, and the ceiling decorations painted for the Etruscan Gallery of the Louvre in 1952–3, are among the earliest examples of Braque's work in this late vein; although it was not until 1956 that the bird-and-sky theme became the principal subject of his canvases. In the summer of the previous year Braque had visited the Camargue where his friend Lukas Hoffmann owned a bird sanctuary, and the experience of watching flamingos and white egrets flying across the huge skies of the Rhône Delta moved him deeply and strengthened a fascination already planted in him for wastes of plain, water and sky, whose very emptiness seemed a substance to be touched; and for the image of the bird whose purposeful flight mapped out that emptiness, gave it direction and meaning, bore with it on its journey the feelings and dreams of the artist.

On the Wing and *Bird returning to its Nest,* both 1956, are among the outstanding paintings which Braque executed on this theme. In the first an ice-blue sky has been painstakingly built up into a thick impasto in such a way that open space is described not as an illusion of infinite depth but as an actual material resting between the spectator and the canvas. Across that material a bird darts towards a dark object which represents nothing specific but which becomes in later paintings (such as the more romantic *Night Flight* of 1958) the image of the moon. Another puzzle which Braque subsequently added to *On the Wing* is the boxed-off picture-within-a-picture at the bottom left, representing a second bird in flight.

Ills. 156, 149

Ill. 152

152 *Night Flight* 1957–8

In *Bird returning to its Nest,* which Braque chose to represent him at the World Fair of 1958, the light and dark areas are reversed, the sky now being a deep brown impasto which even more strongly emphasizes its material nature, while the bird gliding across it is pale buff. Here Braque has added the image of a nest with eggs (repeated in several later paintings such as *Ill. 150*), but he has continued to treat the theme with the same dispassion he would give to a still-life. Not a grain of sentimentality sweetens the austerity of the composition.

A pall of private meaning hangs over these *Bird* paintings, and in the final issue it is a meaning so personal that one may sense and guess at it but scarcely define it. It may be that the appeal of Braque's late work springs from this mystery, as well as from its apparent isolation from the remainder of his work

200

153 *Bird returning to its Nest* 1959

154 *The Black Boat* 1958

This small grey painting hung in Braque's house in Paris until his death. It is one of a number of paintings never publicly exhibited until 1967.

155 *The Plough* 1959–60

156 *On the Wing* (final state) 1956–61

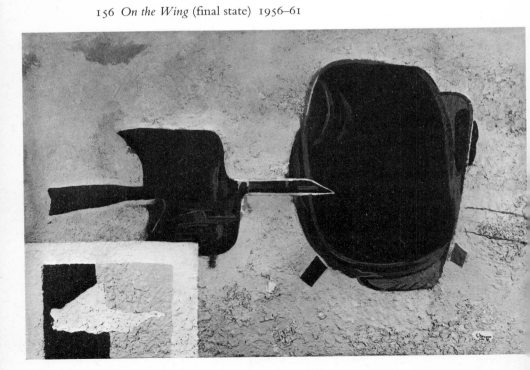

157 *Still-Life with Jug and Grapes* 1960

158 *Bird in the Foliage* 1961

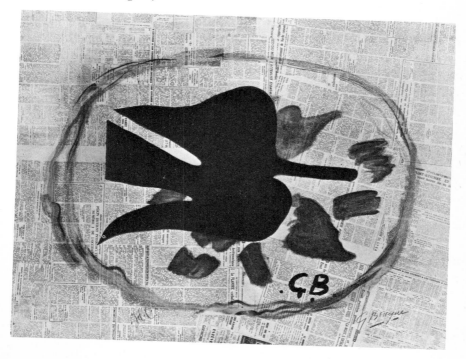

and the work of any other twentieth-century painter (except – in the case of the lithographs – Matisse).

Very much the same feeling of a private significance applies to another, more naturalistic group of paintings, contemporary with the *Bird* pictures: those which treat in an atmospheric and almost Impressionistic manner objects abandoned on a beach or in the fields: *The Plough* of 1959–60, *The Belgian Plough* of 1962, and *The Weeding Machine* of 1961–3 which was Braque's last completed canvas, or that little gem in grey which remained in his studio until his death, *The Black Boat* of 1958. Going back further in time one might happily include in this group *Boats on the Beach* of 1949.

Ills. 155, 15

Ill. 160

Ill. 154

Ill. 123

Like all his work since Fauvism these paintings are about *things,* the physical nature and presence of things; but they are also paintings in which ultimately Braque has come to terms with objects that belong in a natural setting, that belong intimately to landscape, that are affected by its light, its climate and its moods. Braque's skies are now heavy with storm. His fields reflect the sparkle of sunlight, give out the smell of heat and of harvest.

In the end Braque has drawn closer not so much to the Impressionists as to Van Gogh; and, as in Van Gogh, Braque's images are the more memorable for having, so to speak, absorbed the personality and passions of the artist. All his life Braque chose to paint those objects most familiar to him and most loved by him. By the end it is almost as though he actually became those objects: the bicycle on which as a young man he used to cycle home to Le Havre from Paris, the bird returning to its nest, the machinery disused in a field, the old boat resting on the shore.

◄ 159 *The Belgian Plough* 1962

◄ 160 *The Weeding Machine* 1961–3

The artist's last completed painting.

Selective Bibliography

Statements by the artist

'Pensées et Réflexions sur la Peinture', in *Nord-Sud* No. 10, Paris 1917.
Cahier de Georges Braque 1917–47, Paris 1947, supplement 1956.
'Braque, La Peinture et Nous', statements made to Dora Vallier, in *Cahiers d'Art*, Paris 1954.
G. DIEHL, 'L'Univers Pictural et son Destin', in *Les Problèmes de la Peinture*, Paris 1945.
J. RICHARDSON, 'The Power of Mystery', in *The Observer*, 1 December 1957, London.
E. TÉRIADE, 'Braque parle', in *Verve*, Vol. VII, Paris 1952.
G. CHARBONNIER, 'Braque', in *Le Monologue du Peintre*, Paris 1959.

Books

G. APOLLINAIRE, *Les Peintres Cubistes*, Paris 1913, New York 1944.
A. BARR, *Cubism and Abstract Art*, New York 1936.
R. BISSIÈRE, *G. Braque*, Paris 1920.
P. CABANNE, *L'Epopée du Cubisme*, Paris 1963.
D. COOPER, *Braque: Paintings 1909–47*, London 1948.
D. COOPER (ed.), *Letters of Juan Gris,* London 1956.
G. DUTHUIT, *Les Fauves*, Geneva 1949.
C. EINSTEIN, *G. Braque*, Paris 1934.
E. FRY, *Cubism*, London 1966.
S. FUMET, *Braque*, Paris 1945.
Sculptures de G. Braque, Paris 1951.
A. E. GALLATIN, *Georges Braque*, New York 1943.
M. GIEURE, *G. Braque*, Paris 1956.
J. GOLDING, *Cubism: A History and an Analysis*, London 1959.
P. HERON, *Braque*, London 1958.
W. HOFMANN, *Georges Braque: his lithographic work*, London 1962.

H. R. HOPE, *Georges Braque*, New York 1949.
G. JANNEAU, *L'Art Cubiste*, Paris 1929.
D.-H. KAHNWEILER (under pseudonym D. HENRY), *Der Weg zum Kubismus*, Munich 1926, New York 1949.
J. LEYMARIE, *Braque*, Geneva 1961.
F. MOURLOT, *Braque: lithographe*, Monte Carlo 1963.
F. OLIVIER, *Picasso et ses Amis*, Paris 1933, reprinted 1955.
J. PAULHAN, *Braque le Patron*, Paris 1945.
F. PONGE, *Braque le Réconciliateur*, Geneva 1946.
M. RAYNAL, *G. Braque*, Rome and Paris 1923.
P. REVERDY, *Braque*, Paris 1949.
J. RICHARDSON, *Georges Braque*, London 1959.
G. Braque, London 1962.
J. RUSSELL, *G. Braque*, London 1959.
A. SALMON, *L'Art Vivant*, Paris 1920.
C. STERLING, *Still Life Painting from Antiquity to the Present Day*, Paris 1959.
A. VERDET, *G. Braque*, Geneva and Monaco 1956.
Georges Braque le solitaire, Paris 1959.
C. ZERVOS, *Histoire de l'Art Contemporain*, Paris 1938.
Georges Braque: nouvelles sculptures et plaques gravées, Paris 1960.

Catalogues

E. ENGELBERTS, *Georges Braque: œuvre Graphique original*, Geneva 1958.
L'œuvre Graphique de Georges Braque, Lausanne 1962.
G. ISARLOV, *Georges Braque*, Paris 1932.
N. MANGIN (ed.), *Catalogue de l'œuvre de Georges Braque* (in process of publication), Paris. 1922–27, 1928–35, 1936–41, 1942–47, 1948–57 have already appeared.

List of Illustrations

Sizes are given in inches, height preceding width. A few dates are questionable. Mostly I have followed the *catalogue raisonné* being prepared by the Galerie Maeght.

1 Photograph of Georges Braque, by kind permission of John Russell

2 *Breton Girl*, 1903–4
Signed
Oil on canvas, $21\frac{5}{8} \times 18$
Collection: Herr M. Rosensaft
Photo: Galerie Maeght

3 *View of the Park at Honfleur*, 1904–5
Signed
Oil on canvas, $19\frac{3}{4} \times 23\frac{5}{8}$
Collection: Nouveau Musée des Beaux-Arts, Le Havre
Photo: Nouveau Musée des Beaux-Arts, Le Havre

4 *Boats*, 1901–5
Signed
Oil on canvas, $13\frac{1}{4} \times 18\frac{1}{8}$
Collection: M. Jean Paulhan
Photo: Galerie Maeght

5 *Ship in Harbour, Le Havre*, 1905
Signed
Oil on canvas, $21\frac{1}{4} \times 25\frac{1}{2}$
Collection: E. & A. Silberman Galleries, New York
Photo: Galerie Maeght

6 *The Mast, Antwerp*, 1906
Unsigned
Oil on canvas, $18\frac{1}{8} \times 13$
Private collection
Photos: Galerie Maeght

7 *Le Mas*, 1906
Signed
Oil on canvas, $19\frac{3}{4} \times 24$
Private collection
Photo: Galerie Louise Leiris

8 *At L'Estaque*, 1906
Signed
Oil on canvas, $19\frac{1}{4} \times 24$
Private collection, Paris
Photo: Galerie Maeght

9 *L'Estaque, L'Embarcadère*, 1906
Signed and dated
Oil on canvas, $14\frac{1}{2} \times 18\frac{1}{8}$
Collection: Musée National d'Art Moderne, Paris
Photo: Service de Documentation Photographique des Musées Nationaux, Réunion des Musées Nationaux

10 *The Little Bay at La Ciotat*, 1907
Signed
Oil on canvas, $15 \times 18\frac{1}{4}$
Collection: Mr and W. E. Josten, New York
Photo: Galerie Maeght

11 *Port of Antwerp*, 1906
Unsigned
Oil on canvas, $19\frac{3}{4} \times 24$
Collection: Kunstmuseum, Basle
Photo: Galerie Maeght

12 *Landscape at L'Estaque*, 1907
Unsigned
Oil on canvas, $25\frac{1}{2} \times 31\frac{7}{8}$
Private collection
Photo: Galerie Maeght

13 *La Ciotat*, 1907
Signed
Oil on canvas, $23\frac{1}{4} \times 23\frac{3}{8}$
Private collection
Photo: Galerie Maeght

14 *Hills at La Ciotat*, 1907
Originally signed on the back, now relined
Oil on canvas, $28 \times 23\frac{1}{2}$
Private collection
Photo: Galerie Maeght

15 *View from the Hôtel Mistral, L'Estaque*, 1907
Signed on the back
Oil on canvas, $31\frac{1}{2} \times 23\frac{5}{8}$
Collection: Mr and W. E. Josten, New York
Photo: Galerie Maeght

16 *Houses at L'Estaque*, 1908
Signed on back
Oil on canvas, $28\frac{3}{4} \times 23\frac{3}{8}$
Collection: Hermann and Margrit Rupf
Foundation, Musée des Beaux-Arts de Berne
Photo: Galerie Maeght

17 *Nude*, 1907–8
Signed (after this photograph was taken)
Oil on canvas, $55\frac{3}{4} \times 40$
Ex-collection: Mme Cuttoli, Paris
Photo: Galerie Maeght

18 *Nude*, 1908
Unsigned
Etching, $11 \times 7\frac{3}{4}$
Edition of 25 on Auvergne, 30 on Arches;
published in 1953
Photo: Galerie Maeght

19 *Les Demoiselles d'Avignon*, 1907, by Pablo
Picasso (born 1881)
Oil on canvas, 96×92
Collection: Museum of Modern Art, New
York
Photo: Museum of Modern Art, New York

20 *Trees (at L'Estaque)*, 1908
Unsigned
Oil on canvas, $28\frac{3}{4} \times 23\frac{3}{8}$
Collection: Museum of Copenhagen
Photo: Galerie Maeght

21 *Landscape at L'Estaque*, 1908
Unsigned
Oil on canvas, $31\frac{7}{8} \times 25\frac{1}{2}$
Collection: Kunstmuseum, Basle
Photo: Galerie Maeght

22 *The Mandolin*, 1910
Signed on back
Oil on canvas, $28\frac{1}{2} \times 23\frac{1}{2}$
Collection: Tate Gallery, London
Photo: Sotheby and Co. Ltd

23 *Still-Life with Violin and Glass*, 1913
Signed on back
Oil on canvas $32\frac{1}{4} \times 24\frac{1}{8}$
Collection: Württembergische Staatsgalerie,
Stuttgart

24 *Still-Life with Fruit-dish and Plate*, 1908
Unsigned
Oil on canvas, $18\frac{1}{8} \times 21\frac{1}{4}$
Collection: Mr and Mrs Hans Arnold, New
York
Photo: Galerie Maeght

25 *Musical Forms*, 1913
Oil, pencil and charcoal on canvas, $36\frac{1}{4} \times 25\frac{5}{8}$
Collection: Philadelphia Museum of Art

26 *Woman with a Guitar*, 1913
Oil on canvas, $51\frac{1}{8} \times 29\frac{1}{8}$
Collection: Musée National d'Art Moderne,
Paris

27 *Harbour in Normandy*, 1909
Unsigned
Oil on canvas, 32×32
Collection: Mr Walter P. Chrysler, Jr,
New York, U.S.A.
Photo: Galerie Maeght

28 *The Clarinet*, 1913
Unsigned
Pasted paper, charcoal and oil on paper,
$39\frac{3}{8} \times 51\frac{1}{4}$
Private collection
Photo: Galerie Maeght

29 *Glass, Bottle and Newspaper*, 1913
Signed on back
Pasted paper and charcoal on paper, $24\frac{5}{8} \times 11\frac{1}{4}$
Private collection, Basle
Photo: Galerie Maeght

30 *Village of Gardanne*, 1885, by Paul Cézanne
(1839–1906)
Oil on canvas
Collection: Brooklyn Museum

31 *La Roche-Guyon, The Château*, 1909
Signed on the back
Oil on canvas, $31\frac{3}{4} \times 23\frac{1}{2}$
Collection: M. Rolf de Maré, Stockholm
Photo: Galerie Maeght

32 *La Roche-Guyon, The Château*, 1909
Signed on the back
Oil on canvas, $36\frac{1}{4} \times 28\frac{3}{4}$
Collection: Museum of Eindhoven, Holland
Photo: Galerie Maeght

33 *Guitar and Fruit-dish*, 1909
Unsigned
Oil on canvas, $21\frac{1}{2} \times 15$
Collection: Hermann and Margrit Rupf
Foundation, Musée des Beaux-Arts de Berne
Photo: Musée des Beaux-Arts de Berne

34 *View of Montmartre (with the Sacré-Cœur) from
the Artist's Studio*, 1910
Signed on back
Oil on canvas, $21\frac{5}{8} \times 16$
Private collection
Photo: Galerie Louise Leiris

35   *Violin and Pitcher*, 1910
Unsigned
Oil on canvas, $45\frac{5}{8} \times 29$
Collection: Kunstmuseum, Basle
Photo: Galerie Louise Leiris

36   *Violin and Palette*, 1910
Unsigned
Oil on canvas, $35\frac{7}{8} \times 16\frac{5}{8}$
Collection: Solomon   R.   Guggenheim
Museum, New York
Photo: Galerie Maeght

37   *Piano and Lute*, 1910
Unsigned
Oil on canvas, $36\frac{1}{8} \times 16\frac{7}{8}$
Collection: Solomon   R.   Guggenheim
Museum, New York
Photo: Solomon R. Guggenheim Museum,
New York

38   *Glass on a Table*, 1910
Signed (after this photograph was taken)
Oil on canvas, $13\frac{3}{4} \times 15\frac{1}{4}$
Collection: Sir Antony Hornby
Photo: Galerie Maeght

39   *Woman with a Mandolin*, 1910
Signed
Oil on canvas, $36 \times 28\frac{1}{2}$
Private collection, Switzerland
Photo: Sotheby and Co. Ltd

40   *Violin and Glass*, 1910–11
Unsigned
Oil on canvas, $20 \times 26\frac{1}{4}$
Collection: National Gallery, Prague
Photo: National Gallery, Prague

41   *Portrait of Daniel-Henry Kahnweiler*, 1910, by
Pablo Picasso (born 1881)
Oil on canvas, $39\frac{5}{8} \times 28\frac{5}{8}$
Collection: The Art Institute of Chicago
Photo: The Art Institute of Chicago

42   *The Portuguese*, 1911
Signed on back
Oil on canvas, $45\frac{7}{8} \times 32$
Collection: Kunstmuseum, Basle
Photo: Kunstmuseum, Basle

43   *Still-Life with Violin*, 1910–11
Unsigned
Oil on canvas, $51\frac{1}{8} \times 35\frac{1}{2}$
Collection: Musée National d'Art Moderne,
Paris
Photo: Service de Documentation Photo-
graphique des Musées Nationaux, Réunion
des Musées Nationaux

44   *Woman Reading*, 1911
Signed on back
Oil on canvas, $50\frac{3}{4} \times 31\frac{7}{8}$
Ex-collection: M. Raoul La Roche, Paris
Photo: Galerie Maeght

45   *Fox*, 1911
Unsigned
Etching, $21\frac{1}{2} \times 14\frac{5}{8}$
Edition of 100 on Arches
Photo: Galerie Maeght

46   *The Guéridon*, 1911
Signed on back
Oil on canvas, $45\frac{5}{8} \times 31\frac{7}{8}$
Collection: Musée National d'Art Moderne,
Paris
Photo: Galerie Louise Leiris

47   *Man with a Violin*, 1911–12
Oil on canvas, $39\frac{1}{4} \times 28$
Collection: Herr E. Bührle, Zürich
Photo: Herr E. Bührle, Zürich

48   *Still-Life with Dice, Pipe and Glasses*, 1911–12
Signed on back
Oil on canvas, $28\frac{5}{8} \times 20\frac{3}{4}$
Collection: Mrs R. Eichholz
Photo: Galerie Maeght

49   *Homage to J. S. Bach*, 1912
Signed on back
Oil on canvas, $21\frac{1}{4} \times 28\frac{3}{4}$
Private collection
Photo: Galerie Maeght

50   *Fruit-dish and Glass*, 1912
Signed (after this photograph was taken)
Pasted paper and charcoal on paper, $24 \times 17\frac{1}{2}$
Private collection
Photo: Galerie Maeght

51   *Still-Life with a Bunch of Grapes*, 1912
Signed on back
Oil on canvas, $28\frac{3}{4} \times 23\frac{5}{8}$
Private collection
Photo: Galerie Louise Leiris

52   *Aria de Bach*, 1913
Signed
Pasted paper and charcoal on paper, $24\frac{1}{2} \times 18\frac{1}{4}$
Collection: Mme Cuttoli, Paris
Photo: Galerie Maeght

53   *The Cinema Programme*, 1913
Unsigned
Pasted paper and charcoal on canvas, $36\frac{5}{8} \times 25\frac{5}{8}$
Private collection
Photo: Galerie Louise Leiris

54 *Still-Life with Playing Cards*, 1913
Signed on back
Oil and charcoal on canvas, $32 \times 23\frac{5}{8}$
Collection: Musée National d'Art Moderne,
Paris
Photo: Galerie Louise Leiris

55 *Bottle and Glass*, 1913
Signed on back
Oil on canvas, $15 \times 21\frac{5}{8}$
Private collection, Zürich
Photo: Galerie Maeght

56 *Glass and Violin*, 1913–14
Signed on back
Oil, pasted paper and charcoal on canvas,
$31\frac{3}{4} \times 45\frac{5}{8}$
Collection: Kunstmuseum, Basle
Photo: Kunstmuseum, Basle

57 *Music*, 1914
Signed (in imitation of name-plate)
Oil on canvas with gesso and sawdust, $36 \times 23\frac{1}{2}$
Phillips Collection, Washington, D.C.
Photo: French National Photographic
Archives

58 *The Bottle of Rum*, 1914
Unsigned
Oil and charcoal on canvas, $18\frac{1}{8} \times 21\frac{1}{2}$
Collection: Comte de Beaumont
Photo: Galerie Maeght

59 *The Guitar*, 1917
Signed on the back
Oil on canvas, $23\frac{5}{8} \times 39\frac{3}{8}$
Collection: Rijksmuseum Kröller-Müller,
Otterlo
Photo: French National Photographic
Archives

60 *The Musician*, 1917–18
Signed
Oil on canvas, $86\frac{3}{4} \times 44\frac{3}{4}$
Collection: Kunstmuseum, Basle
Photo: French National Photographic
Archives

61 *Guitar and Clarinet*, 1918
Unsigned
Pasted paper, corrugated cardboard, charcoal
and gouache on cardboard, $30\frac{3}{8} \times 37\frac{3}{8}$
Collection: Philadelphia Museum, Arensberg
collection
Photo: French National Photographic
Archives

62 *Clarinet, Guitar and Fruit-dish*, 1918
Signed on back
Oil on canvas, $28\frac{3}{4} \times 39\frac{3}{8}$
Collection: Kunstmuseum, Basle
Photo: French National Photographic
Archives

63 *Café-Bar*, 1919
Signed on back
Oil and sand on canvas, $63 \times 32\frac{1}{4}$
Collection: Kunstmuseum, Basle
Photo: Kunstmuseum, Basle

64 *The Black Guéridon*, 1919
Signed on back
Oil and sand on canvas, $29\frac{1}{2} \times 51\frac{1}{8}$
Collection: Musée National d'Art Moderne,
Paris
Photo: French National Photographic
Archives

65 *Woman with a Mandolin*, 1917
Unsigned
Oil on canvas, $36\frac{1}{4} \times 25\frac{5}{8}$
Private collection
Photo: Galerie Maeght

66 *Anemones*, 1924
Signed and dated
Oil and sand on canvas, $11\frac{5}{8} \times 13\frac{1}{2}$
Private collection, Paris
Photo: Galerie Maeght

67 *Still-Life with Guitar*, 1921
Unsigned
Oil on canvas, $51 \times 29\frac{1}{2}$
Collection: National Gallery, Prague
Photo: National Gallery, Prague

68 *The Mantelpiece*, 1921
Signed on back
Oil on canvas, $51\frac{1}{8} \times 29\frac{1}{8}$
Collection: Mr and Mrs Richard K. Weil, St
Louis, Mo., U.S.A.
Photo: Galerie Louise Leiris

69 *Portrait of Christine Nilsson*, 1874, by Jean-
Baptiste Camille Corot (1796–1875)
Oil on canvas, $31\frac{1}{2} \times 22\frac{1}{2}$
Collection: Museu de Arte, São Paulo

70 *Souvenir de Corot*, 1922–3
Signed with initials above 'Corot'
Oil on canvas, $16\frac{1}{8} \times 13$
Collection: Musée National d'Art Moderne,
Paris
Photo: Réunion des Musées Nationaux

71 *Canephorus*, 1922–3
Signed
Oil and sand on canvas, $70\frac{3}{4} \times 28\frac{1}{2}$
Collection: Musée National d'Art Moderne, Paris
Photo: Galerie Maeght

72 *Canephorus*, 1922–3
Signed
Oil and sand on canvas, $70\frac{3}{4} \times 28\frac{1}{2}$
Collection: Musée National d'Art Moderne, Paris
Photo: Galerie Maeght

73 *Sill-Life with Guitar and Fruit*, 1924
Signed
Oil and sand on canvas, $45\frac{1}{2} \times 23\frac{1}{2}$
Private collection
Photo: Galerie Maeght

74 *Bottle, Glass and Fruit*, 1924
Signed
Oil and sand on board, $20\frac{1}{8} \times 21\frac{5}{8}$
Collection: Lord Amulree, London
Photo: Galerie Maeght

75 *Reclining Nude*, 1924
Signed
Oil on board, $11\frac{3}{4} \times 23\frac{3}{4}$
Ex-collection: E. Bührle, Zürich
Photo: Galerie Maeght

76 *Reclining Nude*, 1925
Signed and dated
Oil on canvas, $9\frac{1}{8} \times 21\frac{1}{2}$
Ex-collection: E. Bührle, Zürich
Photo: Marlborough Fine Art, London

77 *Nude with Basket of Fruit*, 1925
Signed
Oil and canvas, $36\frac{1}{4} \times 28\frac{3}{4}$
Collection: Mr and Mrs Arnold, Maremont, Winnetka, Illinois, U.S.A.
Photo: Galerie Maeght

78 *Bather*, 1925
Signed
Oil on board, $26\frac{3}{8} \times 21\frac{5}{8}$
Collection: Tate Gallery, London
Photo: Tate Gallery, London

79 *The Guéridon, c.* 1928
Signed
Oil and sand on canvas
Private collection, Garches
Photo: Galerie Maeght

80 *Mandolin, Glass, Pot and Fruit*, 1927
Oil on canvas, $31\frac{7}{8} \times 45\frac{3}{4}$
Collection: Tate Gallery, London
Photo: Tate Gallery, London

81 *The Bottle of Marc*, 1930
Signed
Oil and sand on canvas, $51\frac{1}{8} \times 29\frac{1}{8}$
Private collection
Photo: Galerie Maeght

82 *Still-Life*, 1925
Signed
Oil on board, $15\frac{3}{4} \times 23\frac{5}{8}$
Collection: Tate Gallery, London
Photo: Tate Gallery, London

83 *The Marble Table*, 1925
Signed
Oil on canvas, $51\frac{1}{2} \times 29$
Collection: Musée National d'Art Moderne, Paris
Photo: Galerie Maeght

84 *Still-Life with Fruit*, 1926
Signed
Oil on canvas, $18\frac{7}{8} \times 23$
Collection: Glasgow City Art Gallery and Museum
Photo: Galerie Maeght

85 *The Black Rose*, 1927
Signed
Oil on canvas, 20×36
Collection: Mrs Burton Tremaine, Jr, Meriden, Conn., U.S.A.
Photo: Galerie Maeght

86 *Table, Fruit and Jug*, 1926
Signed
Oil on canvas, $31\frac{7}{8} \times 39\frac{3}{4}$
Collection: Mr and Mrs Charles Pomaret, Nice
Photo: Galerie Maeght

87 *Guitar, Fruit and Pitcher*, 1927
Signed
Oil and sand on canvas, 29×36
Collection: Mr and Mrs Lincoln Schuster, New York, U.S.A.
Photo: Galerie Maeght

88 *Head I*, 1928
Signed
Oil on canvas, $18\frac{1}{8} \times 15$
Collection: Mr Edward Bragaline, New York, U.S.A.
Photo: Galerie Maeght

89 *The Guéridon*, 1928–9
Signed
Oil over gesso on canvas, $57\frac{1}{2} \times 44\frac{3}{4}$
The Phillips Collection, Washington, D.C.,
U.S.A.
Photo: Galerie Maeght

90 *The Large Table*, 1929
Signed
Oil over gesso on canvas, $45\frac{1}{4} \times 57\frac{3}{4}$
Chester Dale Collection, U.S.A.
Photo: Galerie Maeght

91 *The Guéridon* (detail of 89)

92 *Fruit-dish with pears*, 1930
Signed and dated
Oil on canvas, $15\frac{3}{8} \times 21\frac{5}{8}$
Collection: Marlborough Fine Art Ltd,
London
Photo: Marlborough Fine Art Ltd, London

93 *Large Brown Still-Life*, 1931–2
Signed
Oil on canvas, $51\frac{1}{8} \times 76\frac{3}{4}$
Private collection, France
Photo: Galerie Maeght

94 *Boats on the Beach, Dieppe*, 1929
Signed
Oil on canvas, $19\frac{3}{4} \times 25\frac{5}{8}$
Collection: Herr W. Schniewind, Neviges
Photo: Galerie Maeght

95 *The Blue Mandolin* (*The Blue Guitar*), 1930
Signed
Oil over gesso on canvas, $45\frac{1}{2} \times 35$
Collection: City Art Museum, St Louis,
U.S.A.
Photo: Galerie Maeght

96 *The Grey Table*, 1930
Signed
Oil on canvas, $57 \times 29\frac{7}{8}$
Private collection, New York, U.S.A.
Photo: Galerie Maeght

97 *The Clay Pipe*, 1931
Signed
Oil on canvas, $10\frac{5}{8} \times 13\frac{3}{4}$
Private collection
Photo: Galerie Maeght

98 *A Nereid*, 1931–2
Unsigned
Incised plaster, $73\frac{5}{8} \times 51\frac{1}{8}$
Collection: Aimé Maeght
Photo: Galerie Maeght

99 *The White Tablecloth*, by Jean-Baptiste Siméon
Chardin (1699–1779)
Oil on canvas, $37\frac{7}{8} \times 48\frac{3}{4}$
Collection: The Art Institute of Chicago
Photo: The Royal Academy of Arts, London

100 *The Yellow Tablecloth*, 1935
Unsigned
Oil and sand on canvas, 45×57
Collection: Mr and Mrs Samuel A. Marx,
Chicago, U.S.A.
Photo: Galerie Maeght

101 *Still-Life on a Printed Tablecloth*, 1935
Signed
Oil on canvas, $28\frac{3}{4} \times 36\frac{1}{4}$
Collection: Metropolitan Museum of Art,
New York, U.S.A.
Photo: Galerie Maeght

102 *Still-Life with Mandolin*, 1936
Signed
Oil on canvas, $38\frac{1}{4} \times 51\frac{1}{8}$
Private collection, U.S.A.
Photo: Galerie Maeght

103 *Still-Life with Fruit-dish*, 1936
Signed (after this photograph was taken)
Oil on canvas, $25\frac{5}{8} \times 31\frac{3}{4}$
Collection: Mrs S.S. White III and Vera
White, Ardmore, Pennsylvania, U.S.A.
Photo: Galerie Maeght

104 *Woman with an Easel*, 1936
Signed
Oil on canvas, $36\frac{1}{4} \times 28\frac{3}{4}$
Collection: Mr Nathan Cummings, Chicago
Photo: Galerie Maeght

105 *The Duet*, 1937
Signed
Oil and sand on canvas, $51\frac{1}{8} \times 63$
Collection: Musée National d'Art Moderne,
Paris
Photo: Galerie Maeght

106 *Blue Boats*, 1937
Signed
Oil on panel, 9×13
Collection: Marlborough Fine Art Ltd,
London
Photo: Marlborough Fine Art Ltd

107 *The Cliffs*, 1938
Signed
Oil on canvas, $20 \times 25\frac{1}{2}$
Collection: Mr and Mrs Leigh B. Block,
Chicago, U.S.A.
Photo: Galerie Maeght

108 *Vanitas I*, 1938
Signed
Oil on canvas, $21\frac{1}{4} \times 25\frac{1}{2}$
Private collection
Photo: Galerie Maeght

109 *The Painter and his Model*, 1939
Unsigned
Oil on canvas, 50×70
Collection: Mr Walter P. Chrysler, Jr, New York, U.S.A.
Photo: Galerie Maeght

110 *Still-Life with Garden Chair*, 1939
Signed
Oil on canvas, $25\frac{5}{8} \times 31\frac{1}{2}$
Collection: Mrs Mark C. Steinberg, St Louis, U.S.A.
Photo: Galerie Maeght

111 *In Front of the Window*, 1942
Signed
Oil on canvas, $51\frac{3}{4} \times 38\frac{1}{2}$
Collection: Musée National d'Art Moderne, Paris
Photo: Réunion des Musées Nationaux

112 *Patience*, 1942
Signed
Oil and sand on canvas, $57\frac{1}{8} \times 44\frac{1}{2}$
Private collection
Photo: Galerie Maeght

113 *The Black Fish*, 1942
Signed
Oil on canvas, $13 \times 21\frac{5}{8}$
Collection: Musée National d'Art Moderne, Paris
Photo: Galerie Maeght

114 *Interior: The Grey Table*, 1942
Signed
Oil and sand on canvas, $55\frac{1}{8} \times 77\frac{1}{8}$
Private collection, U.S.A.
Photo: Galerie Maeght

115 *Jug and Skull*, 1943
Signed
Oil on canvas, $16\frac{7}{8} \times 29$
Collection: Saarland Museum, Saarbrücken
Photo: Galerie Maeght

116 *The Kitchen Table*, 1942–4
Signed
Oil and sand on canvas, $51\frac{1}{4} \times 29$
Collection: Herr Gustav Zumsteg, Zürich
Photo: Galerie Maeght

117 *The Salon*, 1944
Signed
Oil and sand on canvas, $47\frac{1}{4} \times 59$
Collection: Musée National d'Art Moderne, Paris
Photo: Galerie Maeght

118 *Billiard-Table I*, 1944
Signed
Oil and sand on canvas, $51\frac{1}{4} \times 76\frac{1}{2}$
Collection: Musée National d'Art Moderne, Paris
Photo: Galerie Maeght

119 *The Billiard-Table*, 1944–52
Signed
Oil and sand on canvas, $76\frac{1}{4} \times 38\frac{1}{4}$
Collection: M. Jacques Gellman, Mexico City
Photo: Galerie Maeght

120 *The Little Horse*, 1939
Plaster, $7\frac{7}{8} \times 5\frac{7}{8}$
Collection: Aimé Maeght
Photo: Galerie Maeght

121 *The Pony*, 1939
Bronze, $7\frac{1}{8} \times 7\frac{7}{8}$
Edition of six
Photo: Galerie Maeght

122 *Horse's Head*, 1941–2 (cast in 1944)
Bronze, $37\frac{3}{4}$ long
Edition of six (3 bronze, 3 zinc)
Photo: Galerie Maeght

123 *Boats on the Beach*, 1949
Signed
Oil on canvas, $18\frac{1}{8} \times 24$
Private collection, Geneva
Photo: Galerie Maeght

124 *Studio I*, 1949
Unsigned
Oil on canvas $36\frac{1}{4} \times 28\frac{3}{4}$
Collection: M. Jean-Pierre Guerlain, Paris
Photo: Galerie Maeght

125 *Studio II*, 1949
Signed
Oil on canvas, $51\frac{1}{8} \times 63\frac{3}{4}$
Collection: M. and Mme Niarchos, Paris
Photo: Galerie Maeght

126 *Studio III*, 1949
Signed
Oil on canvas, $56\frac{3}{4} \times 69$
Collection: Dr Paul Hänggi, Basle
Photo: Galerie Maeght

127 *Studio IV*, 1949
Signed
Oil on canvas, $51\frac{1}{8} \times 76\frac{3}{4}$
Collection: Mme Sacher, Basle
Photo: Galerie Maeght

128 *The Purple Tablecloth*, 1936
Signed
Oil and sand on canvas, $38\frac{1}{2} \times 51\frac{1}{2}$
Collection: Mrs Albert D. Lasker, New York,
U.S.A.
Photo: Galerie Maeght

129 *Still-Life with Flowers and Fruit*, 1938-9
Signed
Oil on canvas, $19\frac{3}{4} \times 25\frac{3}{8}$
Private collection
Photo: Sotheby and Co. Ltd

130 *The Studio*, 1939
Signed
Oil and sand on canvas, $45 \times 57\frac{1}{2}$
Private collection, New York, U.S.A.
Photo: Galerie Maeght

131 *Still-Life: Mandolin II*, 1939-40
Signed
Oil on canvas, 20×36
Collection: Marlborough Fine Art Ltd,
London
Photo: Marlborough Fine Art Ltd, London

132 *The Night*, 1951
Signed
Oil on canvas, $64 \times 28\frac{3}{4}$
Collection: Aimé Maeght
Photo: Galerie Maeght

133 *Woman at the Mirror*, 1945
Signed
Oil on canvas, $45\frac{3}{4} \times 35$
Private collection, Switzerland
Photo: Sotheby and Co. Ltd

134 *Helios V, blue-violet*, 1948
Colour lithograph, $20 \times 16\frac{1}{2}$
Published by Kahnweiler

135 *Studio VI*, 1950-1
Signed
Oil and sand on canvas, $51\frac{1}{4} \times 64$
Collection: Foundation Maeght
Photo: Galerie Maeght

136 *Studio IX*, 1952-6
Signed
Oil on canvas, $57\frac{1}{4} \times 57\frac{1}{2}$
Collection: Aimé Maeght
Photo: Galerie Maeght

137 *Hecate II*, 1962-3 (unique replica)
Clip, lapis lazuli, diamonds and gold, $16\frac{1}{2} \times 15\frac{3}{4}$
Collection: Louvre, Paris
Photo: Gimpel Fils Ltd

138 *Hades*, 1962-3 (unique replica)
Clip, diamonds and gold, $17\frac{1}{2} \times 22\frac{3}{4}$
Collection: Louvre, Paris
Photo: Gimpel Fils Ltd

139 *Pelias and Neleus*, 1962-3
Clip, lapis lazuli, gold and diamonds
Collection: Mrs Louis Gimbel
Photo: Gimpel Fils Ltd

140 *Cahier de Georges Braque*, 1916-1947
Published 1947 by Maeght

141 *The Cornfield*, 1951
Signed
Oil on canvas, $14\frac{1}{4} \times 22$
Ex-Zumsteg Collection
Photo: Marlborough Fine Art Ltd, London

142 *Amaryllis*, 1958
Colour etching, $21\frac{1}{8} \times 18$
Published by Maeght

143 *Still-Life on a Table*, 1939-52
Signed
Oil on canvas, $70\frac{7}{8} \times 28\frac{1}{2}$
Collection: Musée National d'Art Moderne,
Paris
Photo: Galerie Maeght

144 *The Shower*, 1952
Signed
Oil on canvas, $14 \times 21\frac{5}{8}$
Phillips Collection, Washington, D.C.,
U.S.A.
Photo: Galerie Maeght

145 *Design for a Ceiling in the Louvre, II*, 1953
Ceiling measurement $118\frac{1}{8} \times 196\frac{7}{8}$
Photo: Galerie Maeght

146 *Leaves, Colour, Light ('état définitif')*, 1954
Coloured lithograph, $38\frac{3}{8} \times 23\frac{3}{4}$
Edition of 75 on Arches
Photo: Redfern Gallery, London

147 *Studio VIII*, 1954-5
Signed
Oil on canvas, $52 \times 77\frac{1}{2}$
Private collection, France
Photo: Galerie Maeght

148   *Ajax*, 1955
Signed
Oil on paper mounted on canvas, $70\frac{1}{8} \times 28\frac{1}{4}$
Collection: Mr and Mrs Samuel Marx,
Chicago
Photo: Galerie Maeght

149   *Bird returning to its Nest*, 1956
Signed
Oil on canvas, $51\frac{1}{4} \times 68\frac{1}{4}$
Collection: Musée National d'Art Moderne,
Paris
Photo: Galerie Maeght

150   *The Nest in the Foliage*, 1958
Signed
Oil on canvas, $44\frac{7}{8} \times 52$
Collection: Aimé Maeght
Photo: Galerie Maeght

151   *Doves (black background)*, 1958
Painted plaster, 4×7
Collection: Aimé Maeght
Photo: Galerie Maeght

152   *Night Flight*, 1957–8
Signed (with initials)
Oil on canvas, $32\frac{1}{4} \times 64\frac{1}{8}$
Collection: Aimé Maeght
Photo: Galerie Maeght

153   *Bird returning to its Nest*, 1959
Signed
Oil on canvas, $10\frac{5}{8} \times 16\frac{1}{8}$
Collection: Dr Jurmand, Paris
Photo: Galerie Maeght

154   *The Black Boat*, 1958
Unsigned
Oil on canvas, $8\frac{5}{8} \times 13$
Collection: M. Claude Laurens, Paris
Photo: Galerie Maeght

155   *The Plough*, 1959–60
Signed
Oil on canvas, $33\frac{1}{4} \times 76\frac{3}{4}$
Ex-collection the Artist
Photo: Galerie Maeght

156   *On the Wing* (final state), 1956–61
Signed
Oil on canvas, $45\frac{1}{4} \times 67\frac{1}{2}$
Collection: Musée National d'Art Moderne,
Paris
Photo: Galerie Maeght

157   *Still-Life with Jug and Grapes*, 1960
Unsigned
Oil on canvas, $9\frac{1}{2} \times 16\frac{1}{8}$
Collection: M. Claude Laurens
Photo: Galerie Maeght

158   *Bird in the Foliage*, 1961
Coloured lithograph, $31\frac{1}{2} \times 41\frac{1}{2}$
Edition of 50 in vélin
Photo: Redfern Gallery, London

159   *The Belgian Plough*, 1962
Unsigned
Oil on canvas, $33 \times 15\frac{3}{4}$
Collection: M. Claude Laurens
Photo: Galerie Maeght

160   *The Weeding Machine*, 1961–3
Signed
Oil on canvas, $48\frac{1}{2} \times 70\frac{1}{2}$
Collection: Musée National d'Art Moderne,
Paris
Photo: Galerie Maeght

Index

Page numbers in italics refer to illustrations